" *And look through Nature up to N*

I do not own an inch of land,
But all I see is mine,—
The orchard and the mowing-fi
The lawns and gardens fine.
The winds my tax-collectors ar
They bring me tithes divine,-
Wild scents and subtle essence
A tribute rare and free;
And, more magnificent than al
My window keeps for me
A glimpse of blue immensity,
A little strip of sea.

Richer am I than he who owns
Great fleets and argosies;
I have a share in every ship
Won by the inland breeze
To loiter on yon airy road
Above the apple-trees.
I freight them with my untold c
Each bears my own picked cr
And nobler cargoes wait for th
Than ever India knew,—
My ships that sail into the East
Across that outlet blue.

Sometimes they seem like living
The people of the sky,—
Guests in white raiment coming
From heaven, which is close b
I call them by familiar names,
As one by one draws nigh,
So white, so light, so spirit-like,
From violet mists they bloom!
The aching wastes of the unknov
Are half reclaimed from gloon
Since on life's hospitable sea
All souls find sailing room.

The sails, like flakes of roseate
Float in upon the mist;
The waves are broken precious s
Sapphire and amethyst,
Washed from celestial basement
By suns unsetting kissed.
Out through the utmost gates of
Past where the gay stars drift,
To the widening Infinite, my sou
Glides on, a vessel swift;
Yet loses not her anchorage,
In yonder azure rift.

Here sit I, as a little child;
The threshold of God's door
Is that clear band of chrysopras
Now the vast temple floor,
The blinding glory of the dome
I bow my head before;
The universe, O God, is home,
In hight or depth, to me;
Yet here upon Thy footstool gre
Content am I to be;
Glad, when is opened to my nee
Some sea-like glimpse of Thee

—*Luc*

MEHETABEL.—(By Lucy Larcom.)—

Mehetabel's knitting lies loose in her hand;
She watches the gold of a broken red brand
That glitters and flashes
And falls into ashes.
The flame that illumines her face
From the cavernous, black fireplace
Brings ever new wonders of color and shade
To flicker about her, and shimmer, and fade.
Does any one guess
Of this maid's loveliness,
That the lonesome and smoky old room seems
bless?

Mehetabel's mother calls out of the gloom,
From a clatter of shovel and kettle and broom,
From her flurry and worry
Of work-a-day hurry:
"Our Hetty sits there in a dream,
With her needles half round to the seam;
With nothing to vex her, and nothing to try h
But never will she set the river afire."
And back to the din
Of iron and tin
One shadow flits out, while another steals in.

Mehetabel's lover through new-fallen snow
So softly has come that the maid does not know
He is standing behind her,
So happy to find her
Alone that he hardly can speak.
A whisper—a flush on her cheek
More lovely than sunset's reflection by far.
"O Hetty," he murmurs, "the white evening s
And the beacon-lights swim
On the ocean's blue rim,
But I see your sweet eyes, and they make the st [dim

Mehetabel's wooer is stalwart and tall;
His figure looms dark on the flame-lighted wall
Outside in pale shadow
Lie pasture and meadow;
Dim roselight is on the white hill;
The sea glimmers purple and chill.
"O Hetty, be mine for the calm and the storm;
Though cold be the wide world, my heart's love
warm.
Knit me into your dream,
And my rude life will seem
Like a beautiful landscape, in June's golden bea

Mehetabel's forehead has gathered a cloud;
A thousand new thoughts to her young bos
crowd;
Her knitting drops lower;
No lover can show her
The way through her mind's lonely maze.
He reads no response in her gaze.
Her heart is a snow-drift where foot never trod;
Love's sun has not wakened a bud on its sod;
And pure as the glow
Of the stars on the snow
Are the glances that up through her long lashes g

Mehetabel's future, an unexplored land,
Spreads vaguely before her, unpeopled and gra
Its wild paths wait lonely
[illegible] footsteps only;

Though flimsy and worthless it seem
To her mother's eye, filled with the dust-motes of
care;
Though it bar up her path from the heart that
beats there
In the gathering gloom,
Breathing odor and bloom [room.
And sweet sense of life through the dusk of the

Mehetabel's dream—you will guess it in vain;
Only halt to herself is unwound the bright skein.
She is but a woman,
As gentle as human;
Yet rooted in hearts fresh as hers
Is the hope that the universe stirs; [zone,
And broad be her thought as life's measureless
Or narrow as self is, it still is her own;
And alone she may dare
What she never would share
With friendship the dearest, or love the most rare.

Mehetabel's answer—it has not been told.
To ashes has fallen the firelight's red gold.
No mother, no lover,
For her, the world over,
The work-a-day jangle is still.
An empty house stands on the hill.
The rafters are cobwebbed, the ceiling is bare;
But always a wraith haunts the carved oaken chair;
And early and late
There's a creak at the gate,
And a wind through the room like the soft sigh of
"Wait!"

Mehetabel—Hetty—the dream of a dream,
The film of a snow-cloud, a star's broken beam,
Were a tangible story
To hers; but the glory
Of ages dims down to a spark,
And dies out at last in the dark,
Among questions unanswered, unrealized dreams.
Still the beautiful cheat of what may be and seems
Flashes up on night's brink,
Where the live embers blink,
And the tales that they mutter we dream that we
think.

—*Atlantic.*

POEMS

BY

LUCY LARCOM.

BOSTON:
FIELDS, OSGOOD, & CO.,
SUCCESSORS TO TICKNOR AND FIELDS.
1869.

UNIVERSITY PRESS: WELCH, BIGELOW, & CO.,
CAMBRIDGE.

Truly yours,
Lucy Larcom

To the Memory

OF

ELIZABETH H. WHITTIER,

THIS BOOK IS DEDICATED

BY ONE

WHO OWES ITS BEST SUGGESTIONS TO THE INSPIRATION OF HER FRIENDSHIP.

THIS is a haunted world. It hath no breeze
But is the echo of some voice beloved:
Its pines have human tones; its billows wear
The color and the sparkle of dear eyes.
Its flowers are sweet with touch of tender hands
That once clasped ours. All things are beautiful
Because of something lovelier than themselves,
Which breathes within them, and will never die.—
Haunted,—but not with any spectral gloom;
Earth is suffused, inhabited by heaven.

These blossoms, gathered in familiar paths,
With dear companions now passed out of sight,
Shall not be laid upon their graves. They live,
Since love is deathless. Pleasure now nor pride
Is theirs in mortal wise, but hallowing thoughts
Will meet the offering, of so little worth,
Wanting the benison death has made divine.

And visible friends link hands with those unseen,
Veiled in immortal light; their love is one.
And, for love's sake, they will accept these waifs,
Laid at their feet with a heart's gratitude,
And sadness that it has no worthier gift.

CONTENTS.

SEASIDE AND HILLSIDE.

CHILD AND WOMAN.

FROM WITHOUT.

WAR-MEMORIES.

MISCELLANEOUS.

DEVOTIONAL.

THE COMING LIFE.

SEASIDE AND HILLSIDE.

HILARY.

HILARY,
Summer calls thee, o'er the sea!
Like white flowers upon the tide,
In and out the vessels glide;
But no wind on all the main
Sends thy blithe soul home again:
Every salt breeze moans for thee,
Hilary!

Hilary,
Welcome Summer's step will be,
Save to those beside whose door
Doleful birds sit evermore
Singing, "Never comes he here,
Who made every season's cheer."
Dull the June that brings not thee,
Hilary!

Hilary,
What strange world has sheltered thee?
Here the soil beneath thy feet
Rang with songs, and blossomed sweet:
Still the blue skies ask of Earth,
Blind and dumb without thy mirth,
Where she hides thy heart of glee,
Hilary!

Hilary,
All things shape a sigh for thee!
O'er the waves, among the flowers,
Through the lapse of odorous hours,
Breathes a lonely, longing sound,
As of something sought, unfound:
Lorn are all things, lorn are we,
Hilary!

Hilary!
Oh, to sail in quest of thee,
On the trade-wind's steady tune,
On the hurrying monsoon,
Far through torrid seas, that lave
Dry, hot sands, — a breathless grave.
Sad as vain the search would be,
Hilary!

Hilary,
Chase the sorrow from the sea!
Summer-heart, bring summer near,
Warm, and fresh, and airy-clear!
Dead thou art not! dead is pain;
Now Earth sees and sings again;
Death, to hold thee, Life must be,
Hilary!

ON THE BEACH.

WE stroll as children, thou and I,
Upon the sandy beach,
With younger children playing nigh;
The surf-boats dance, the ships go by,
Beyond the cape's vague reach.

It is a comfort once to be
Like those young hearts again;
To feel, O friend beloved, with thee,
The broad refreshment of the sea,
In weary soul and brain.

The white feet pattering on the sand,
The wings that dip and rise,
The mower's whistle from the land,
And girlhood's laugh, and murmuring strand,
All blend and harmonize.

And glimmering beach, and plover's flight,
  And that long surge that rolls
Through bands of green and purple light,
Are fairer to our human sight,
  Because of human souls.

Seest thou yon fleet of anchored isles
  Upon the sea-line gray?
My thoughts o'erfloat these murmurous miles,
To land where bygone summer smiles
  On gorge and sheltering bay.

I wander with a spirit there,
  Along the enchanted shore:
We breathe the soft, sea-scented air,
And think no isle is half so fair
  As rocky Appledore.

She turns to me her large, dark eyes:—
  Were ever eyes so true?—
The twilight flushes, fades, and dies;
The beacon flames; the white stars rise
  Across pale gulfs of blue.

Those eyes on earth no longer shine;
  And yet it seems to me
I see their light, O friend, in thine;
They add a tenderness divine
  Unto this tremulous sea.

Seen and unseen are interblent;
  The waves that hither roll
In whiter curves of foam are spent,
And deeper seems the green content
  Of shore, for her sweet soul.

Can love be hid in funeral urn,
  Or shut within the grave?
Life passes, only to return,
In tints that glow, and stars that burn
  Upon the refluent wave.

The land is dearer for the sea,
  The ocean for the shore:
These sands of time too drear would be,
If heaven's unguessed eternity
  Rolled not our feet before.

A SEA GLIMPSE.

HIGH tide, and the year at ebb:
The sea is a dream to-day:
The sky is a gossamer web
Of sapphire, and pearl, and gray:

A veil over rock and boat;
A breath on the tremulous blue,
Where the dim sails lie afloat,
Or, unaware, slip from view.

They veer to the rosy ray;
They dusk to the violet shade;
Like a thought they flit away;
Like a foolish hope, they fade.

But listen! a sudden plash!
A ship is heaving in sight,
With a stir, and a noisy dash
Of the salt foam, seething white.

Tar-grimed and weather-stained,
  The sailors shout from her deck:
Naught of the sky blue-veined,
  Or the dreamy waves they reck.

And the sunburnt girl, who stands
  Where her feet on the wet wrack slip, —
Eyes shaded with lithe, brown hands, —
  She sees but the coming ship.

HANNAH BINDING SHOES.

POOR lone Hannah,
Sitting at the window, binding shoes.
Faded, wrinkled,
Sitting, stitching, in a mournful muse.
Bright-eyed beauty once was she,
When the bloom was on the tree:
Spring and winter,
Hannah's at the window, binding shoes.

Not a neighbor,
Passing nod or answer will refuse,
To her whisper,
"Is there from the fishers any news?"
O, her heart's adrift, with one
On an endless voyage gone!
Night and morning,
Hannah's at the window, binding shoes.

Fair young Hannah,
Ben, the sunburnt fisher, gayly woos:
Hale and clever,
For a willing heart and hand he sues.
May-day skies are all aglow,
And the waves are laughing so!
For her wedding
Hannah leaves her window and her shoes.

May is passing:
Mid the apple boughs a pigeon coos.
Hannah shudders,
For the mild southwester mischief brews.
Round the rocks of Marblehead,
Outward bound, a schooner sped:
Silent, lonesome,
Hannah 's at the window, binding shoes.

'T is November,
Now no tear her wasted cheek bedews.
From Newfoundland
Not a sail returning will she lose,

Whispering hoarsely, "Fishermen,
Have you, have you heard of Ben?"
Old with watching,
Hannah 's at the window, binding shoes.

Twenty winters
Bleach and tear the ragged shore she views.
Twenty seasons: —
Never one has brought her any news.
Still her dim eyes silently
Chase the white sails o'er the sea:
Hopeless, faithful,
Hannah 's at the window, binding shoes.

SKIPPER BEN.

SAILING away!
Losing the breath of the shores in May,
Dropping down from the beautiful bay,
Over the sea-slope vast and gray!
And the skipper's eyes with a mist are blind;
For a vision comes on the rising wind,
Of a gentle face, that he leaves behind,
And a heart that throbs through the fog-bank dim,
Thinking of him.

Far into night
He watches the gleam of the lessening light
Fixed on the dangerous island height,
That bars the harbor he loves from sight.
And he wishes, at dawn, he could tell the tale
Of how they had weathered the southwest gale,
To brighten the cheek that had grown so pale
With a wakeful night among spectres grim, —
Terrors for him.

Yo-heave-yo!
Here's the Bank where the fishermen go.
Over the schooner's sides they throw
Tackle and bait to the deeps below.
And Skipper Ben in the water sees,
When its ripples curl to the light land breeze,
Something that stirs like his apple trees;
And two soft eyes that beneath them swim,
Lifted to him.

Hear the wind roar,
And the rain through the slit sails tear and pour!
"Steady! we'll scud by the Cape Ann shore,
Then hark to the Beverly bells once more!"
And each man worked with the will of ten;
While up in the rigging, now and then,
The lightning glared in the face of Ben,
Turned to the black horizon's rim,
Scowling on him.

Into his brain
Burned with the iron of hopeless pain,
Into thoughts that grapple, and eyes that strain,
Pierces the memory, cruel and vain!

Never again shall he walk at ease,
Under his blossoming apple trees,
That whisper and sway to the sunset breeze,
While the soft eyes float where the sea-gulls skim,
Gazing with him.

How they went down
Never was known in the still old town.
Nobody guessed how the fisherman brown,
With the look of despair that was half a frown,
Faced his fate in the furious night, —
Faced the mad billows with hunger white,
Just within hail of the beacon-light
That shone on a woman sweet and trim,
Waiting for him.

Beverly bells,
Ring to the tide as it ebbs and swells!
His was the anguish a moment tells, —
The passionate sorrow death quickly knells.
But the wearing wash of a lifelong woe
Is left for the desolate heart to know,
Whose tides with the dull years come and go
Till hope drifts dead to its stagnant brim,
Thinking of him.

THE LIGHT–HOUSES.

TWO pale sisters, all alone,
  On an island bleak and bare,
Listening to the breakers' moan,
  Shivering in the chilly air ;
Looking inland towards a hill,
  On whose top one aged tree
Wrestles with the storm-wind's will,
  Rushing, wrathful, from the sea.

Two dim ghosts at dusk they seem,
  Side by side, so white and tall,
Sending one long, hopeless gleam
  Down the horizon's darkened wall.
Spectres, strayed from plank or spar,
  With a tale none lives to tell,
Gazing at the town afar,
  Where unconscious widows dwell.

Two white angels of the sea,
  Guiding wave-worn wanderers home ;

Sentinels of hope they be,
  Drenched with sleet, and dashed with foam,
Standing there in loneliness,
  Fireside joys for men to keep;
Through the midnight slumberless
  That the quiet shore may sleep.

Two bright eyes awake all night
  To the fierce moods of the sea;
Eyes that only close when light
  Dawns on lonely hill and tree.
O kind watchers! teach us, too,
  Steadfast courage, sufferance long!
Where an eye is turned to you,
  Should a human heart grow strong

BITTERSWEET SHADOWS.

OFF we drifted, yesterday,
Till the sea-foam dashed the spray
Of the woodland bittersweet,
Leaning from a sunlit cove
Where amid salt winds it throve,
Swaying to the tide's low beat.

O, the afternoon was fair!
Murmurous echoes swept the air,—
Sigh of pine, and dip of oar:
Every breeze that passed us, went
Laden with some rare wood-scent,
Loitering down the dreamy shore.

And we lingered, loitering too,
Where the heavy cedars threw
Shadows on the water's gold;
Till again in glee afloat,
Like a bird our idle boat
Skimmed the wavelets manifold.

Then, the crystal channel won,
In its deep the shallop shone,
  Sails of silver, prow of pearl:
Hidden ledges brake that dream,
Sucking down the flash and gleam
  Underneath their high-tide swirl.

Free again, broad sunshine found,
Slid the boat on, greenly wound
  With its veil of bittersweet,
Tangling round the sunk rock's edge,
Catching streamers of sea-sedge
  From the sheen beneath our feet.

Anchored in the dusk, a spell
From the folds of twilight fell
  On the bay's black, star-strewn floor.
Awe with that weird glitter crept
Shuddering through our thoughts; we stept
  Gladly on firm land once more,

Trailing home the bittersweet.
Such dim ending was but meet
  For an afternoon so rare.

Was the date of yesterday?
Years since then have slipt away;
  Few such memories they bare.

No to-days like that remain:
Joy is flavored now with pain;
  For the best of all our crew,—
Helmsman, gentlest passenger,—
Lie so still they will not stir,
  Though the sea should drench them through.

So our shallop floats no more
Where the low, vine-tangled shore
  Dips its orange-golden fruit
To the plashing of the wave:
Only white flowers for a grave,
  Now our serious hands will suit.

Still the sun shines, and we drift
Homeward on the current swift,
  Those who went before to meet.
All things beautiful grow sad:
Yet even grief is sometimes glad;—
  Shade us, Life, with bittersweet!

DIVER AND VOYAGER.

"VOYAGER, hast thou ever been down
Where thy boat glides now,
To the roots of the jagged rocks that frown
O'er a death-white brow?

"To the wasted gems that slip away
From the mocking wave,
Where the shark and swordfish grimly play
Round the sailor's grave?"

"No, diver, no! but thy pearls I wear,
As my boat sways here.
Thou hast told of the rock in ambush, there
Never need I steer.

"And because I know that the traitor wave
Must restore the dead,
While I sail to port o'er the shipwrecked brave,
I can feel no dread."

"Light voyager, 't is of humanity
  That I tell my tale."
"Pale diver, that is the same bright sea
  Over which I sail."

THE LEGEND OF SKADI.

THROUGH the leaves of the Edda there rustles a tale
Of Skadi, the daughter of torrent and gale,
Who, leaving her snow-summits, breezy and free,
Went down to be wedded to Njörd of the sea.

Though bright was the ocean as now, in the day
When Vanir and Æsir held nature in sway,
Of gods though her bridegroom was reckoned the third,
In Skadi's new mansion a murmur was heard.

"O Njörd, I am homesick! the gull's tiresome note,
The moan of the breakers, the tide's endless rote,
They hold my eyes sleepless; I never can stay
By the wide-staring ocean. Come, let us away!

"Away to my mountains, my home in the height,
To the glens and the gorges, the summits of light!"

And Njörd could but listen, and go with his bride;
But there for his sea-haunts he drearily sighed.

"O Skadi, come back to the warm, sunny surf!
The beach-sand is smoother than frost-bitten turf;
I like not, at midnight, the wolf's hungry howl,
The bear's stealthy footstep, the shriek of the owl.

"Nine sunsets, my Skadi, from sole love of thee,
I will give to the mountains, if only for three
With me thou wilt linger the blue wave beside;
The billows shall lull thee, my wild one, my
bride!"

Then down the steep gorges went Skadi and Njörd;
Like wind through the pine-woods they swept to the
fiord,
And back in three mornings they hurried again,
Bearing up to the hill-tops the sigh of the main.

So hither and thither awhile swayed the pair:
But Njörd sickened soon of the fresh inland air,
And once, as he scented afar the salt sea,
"No more of the mountains," he shouted, "for me!"

"I am nine times too weary of cavern and cliff;
All the pine-groves of Norway I 'd give for my skiff.
The twilight, that buries the white, solemn hills,
My blood like the coming of Ragnarök chills."

"Three days and three nights are too many for me
To waste on the ocean, O dull Njörd, and thee!"—
And Skadi has buckled her snow-sandals on,
And back to her mountains alone she has gone.

The red, climbing sunrise, the rosy-fringed mist,
Stealing up from the valley, her clear cheek have
kissed;
And over the hill-tops the frosty blue sky
With the joy of its welcome rekindles her eye.

She tightens her bowstring, she bounds from the
rock;
The elves in their caverns her merry voice mock;
The waterfall's rush to the tarn by the crag,
And the leap of the reindeer, behind her both lag.

But still, as she chases the wolf and the boar,
By sounds she is startled, like surf on the shore,

That surge through the forest, and whisper, and
rave ; —
'T is Njörd, who is calling her back to the wave.

And Njörd hears a hill-note borne in on the tide,
When soft through the sunset the lazy waves glide,
Or tranced in the moonlight the weird water
shines ; —
'T is Skadi, whose singing floats down from her
pines.

He calls, but she leaves not her rock-ranges free ;
She chants from her woodlands ; he stays by the
sea :
A wail thrills the harp-strings of heart lost to heart,
Neither happy together, nor joyous apart.

Of sea-god and hill-maid remains not a sign,
Save the marriage of music in billow and pine.
Still sound the Norse mountains, the tide in the
fiord
With the singing of Skadi, the echo of Njörd.

THE OLD SCHOOL-HOUSE.

I PASSED it yesterday again,
  The school-house by the river,
Where you and I were children, Jane,
  And used to glow and shiver
In heats of June, December's frost;
  And where, in rainy weather,
The swollen roadside brook we crossed
  So many times together.

I felt the trickle of the rain
  From your wet ringlets dripping;
I caught your blue eye's twinkle, Jane,
  When we were nearly slipping;
And thought, while you in fear and glee
  Were clinging to my shoulder,
"O, will she trust herself to me,
  When we are ten years older?"

For I was full of visions vain,—
The boy's romantic hunger.
You were the whole school's darling, Jane,
And many summers younger.
Your head a cherub's used to look,
With sunbeams on it lying,
Bent downward to your spelling-book,
For long and hard words prying.

The mountains through the window-pane
Showered over you their glory.
The awkward farm-boy loved you, Jane:
You know the old, old story.
I never watch the sunset now
Upon those misty ranges,
But your bright lips, and cheek, and brow,
Gleam out of all its changes.

I wonder if you see that chain
On memory's dim horizon;
There 's not a lovelier picture, Jane,
To rest even your sweet eyes on.
The Haystacks each an airy tent,
The Notch a gate of splendor;

And river, sky, and mountains blent
In twilight radiance tender.

I wonder, — with a flitting pain, —
If thoughts of me returning,
Are mingled with the mountains, Jane:
I stifle down that yearning. —
A rich man's wife, on you no claim
Have I, lost dreams to rally;
Yet Pemigewasset sings your name
Along its winding valley:

And once I hoped that for us twain
Might fall one calm life-closing;
That Campton hills might guard us, Jane,
In one green grave reposing.
They say the old man's heart is rock:
You never thought so, never!
And, loving you alone, I lock
The school-house door forever!

ELSIE IN ILLINOIS.

"HOME is home, no matter where!"
Sang a happy, youthful pair,
Journeying westward, years ago, —
As they left the April snow
White on Massachusetts' shore;
Left the sea's incessant roar;
Left the Adirondacks, piled
Like the playthings of a child,
On the horizon's eastern bound;
And, the unbroken forests found,
Heard Niagara's sullen call,
Hurrying to his headlong fall,
Like a Titan in distress,
Tearing through the wilderness,
Rending earth apart, in hate
Of the unpitying hounds of fate.

Over Erie's green expanse
Inland wild-fowl weave their dance:

Lakes on lakes, a crystal chain,
Give the clear heaven back again;—
Wampum strung by Manitou,
Lightly as the beaded dew.

Is it wave, or is it shore?—
Greener gleams the prairie-floor,
West and south, one emerald;
Earth untenanted, unwalled.
There, a thread of silent joy,
Winds the grass-hid Illinois.

Bringing comfort unawares
Out of little daily cares,
Here has Elsie lived a year,
Learning well that home is dear,
By the green breadth measureless
Of the outside wilderness,
So unshadowed, so immense!
Garden without path or fence,
Rolling up its billowy bloom
To her low, one-windowed room.

Breath of prairie-flowers is sweet;
But the babv at her feet

Is the sweetest bud to her,
Keeping such a pleasant stir,
On the cabin hearth at play,
While his father turns the hay,
Loads the grain, or binds the stack,
Until sunset brings him back.

Elsie's thoughts awake must keep,
While the baby lies asleep.
Far Niagara haunts her ears;
Mississippi's rush she hears;
Ancient nurses twain, that croon
For her babe their mighty tune,
Lapped upon the prairies wild:
He will be a wondrous child!

Ah! but Elsie's thoughts will stray
Where, a child, she used to play
In the shadow of the pines:
Moss and scarlet-berried vines
Carpeted the granite ledge,
Sloping to the brooklet's edge,
Sweet with violets, blue and white;
While the dandelions, bright

As if Night had spilt her stars,
Shone beneath the meadow-bars.

Could she hold her babe, to look
In that merry, babbling brook, —
See it picturing his eye
As the violet's blue and shy, —
See his dimpled fingers creep
Where the sweet-breathed May-flowers peep
With pale pink anemones,
Out among the budding trees! —
On his soft cheek falls a tear
For the hillside home so dear.

At her household work she dreams;
And the endless prairie seems
Like a broad, unmeaning face
Read through in a moment's space,
Where the smile so fixed is grown,
Better you would like a frown.

Elsie sighs, "We learn too late,
Little things are more than great.

Hearts like ours must daily be
Fed with some kind mystery,
Hidden in a rocky nook,
Whispered from a wayside brook,
Flashed on unexpecting eyes,
In a winged, swift surprise:
Small the pleasure is to trace
Boundlessness of commonplace."

But the south wind, stealing in,
Her to happier moods will win.
In and out the little gate
Creep wild roses delicate:
Fragrant grasses hint a tale
Of the blossomed intervale
Left behind, among the hills.
Every flower-cup mystery fills;
Every idle breeze goes by,
Burdened with life's blissful sigh.

Elsie hums a thoughtful air;
Spreads the table, sets a chair
Where her husband first shall see

Baby laughing on her knee;
While she watches him afar,
Coming with the evening star
Through the prairie, through the sky,
Each as from eternity.

MY MOUNTAIN.

I SHUT my eyes in the snow-fall
  And dream a dream of the hills.
The sweep of a host of mountains,
  The flash of a hundred rills,

For a moment they crowd my vision;
  Then, moving in troops along,
They leave me one still mountain-picture,
  The murmur of one river's song.

'T is the musical Pemigewasset,
  That sings to the hemlock trees
Of the pines on the Profile Mountain,
  Of the stony Face that sees,

Far down in the vast rock-hollows
  The waterfall of the Flume,
The blithe cascade of the Basin,
  And the deep Pool's lonely gloom.

All night, from the cottage-window
  I can hear the river's tune;
But the hushed air gives no answer
  Save the hemlocks' sullen rune.

A lamb's bleat breaks through the stillness,
  And into the heart of night.—
Afar and around, the mountains,
  Veiled watchers, expect the light.

Then up comes the radiant morning
  To smile on their vigils grand.
Still muffled in cloudy mantles
  Do their stately ranges stand?

It is not the lofty Haystacks
  Piled up by the great Notch-Gate,
Nor the glow of the Cannon Mountain,
  That the Dawn and I await,

To loom out of northern vapors;
  But a shadow, a pencilled line,
That grows to an edge of opal
  Where earth-light and heaven-light shine.

Now rose-tints bloom from the purple;
  Now the blue climbs over the green;
Now, bright in its bath of sunshine,
  The whole grand Shape is seen.

Is it one, or unnumbered summits,—
  The Vision so high, so fair,
Hanging over the singing River
  In the magical depths of air?

Ask not the name of my mountain!
  Let it rise in its grandeur lone;
Be it one of a mighty thousand,
  Or a thousand blent in one.

Would a name evoke new splendor
  From its wrapping and folds of light,
Or a line of the weird rock-writing
  Make plainer to mortal sight?

You have lived and learnt this marvel:
  That the holiest joy that came
From its beautiful heaven to bless you,
  Nor needed nor found a name.

Enough, on the brink of the river
  Looking up and away, to know
That the Hill loves the Pemigewasset,
  And broods o'er its murmurous flow.

Perhaps, if the Campton meadows
  Should attract your pilgrim feet
Up the summer road to the mountains,
  You may chance my dream to meet:—

Either mine, or one more wondrous.
  Or perhaps you will look, and say
You behold only rocks and sunshine,
  Be it dying or birth of day.

Though you find but the stones that build it,
  I shall see through the snow-fall still,
Hanging over the Pemigewasset,
  My glorified, dream-crowned Hill.

SONNETS.

I.

THE DISTANT MOUNTAIN-RANGE.

THEY beckon from their sunset domes afar,
Light's royal priesthood, the eternal hills:
Though born of earth, robed of the sky they are;
And the anointing radiance heaven distils
On their high brows, the air with glory fills.
The portals of the west are opened wide;
And lifted up, absolved from earthly ills,
All thoughts, a reverent throng, to worship glide.
The hills interpret heavenly mysteries,
The mysteries of Light, — an open book
Of Revelation: see, its leaves unfold
With crimson borderings, and lines of gold!
Where the rapt reader, though soul-deep his look,
Dreams of a glory deeper than he sees.

II.

THE PRESENCE.

THE mountain statelier lifts his blue-veiled head,
While, drawing near, we meet him face to face.
Here, as on holy ground, we softly tread;
Yet, with a tender and paternal grace,
He gives the wild flowers in his lap a place:
They climb his sides, as fondled infants might,
And wind around him, in a light embrace,
Their summer drapery, pink and clinging white.
Great hearts have largest room to bless the small;
Strong natures give the weaker home and rest:
So Christ took little children to his breast,
And, with a reverence more profound, we fall
In the majestic presence that can give
Truth's simplest message: "'T is by love ye live."

III.

THE FAREWELL.

NOW ends the hour's communion, near and high:
  We have heard whispers from the mountain's
      heart,
And life henceforth is nobler. With a sigh
  Of grateful sadness, let us now depart,
  And seek our lower levels. Rills that start
From this Hill's bosom, there reflect the sky,
  And his deep shadows greener grace impart
To the sweet vale which doth below him lie.
  One farewell glance from far. The hills are fled!
Hid in the folds of yon funereal cloud.
A moment leans the Loftiest from his shroud:—
  "Our thunders cleanse the valley," lo, he saith:
"'T is not alone by smiles that life is fed:
  Awe fills the sanctuary of deep faith."

AT WINNIPESAUKEE.

O SILENT hills across the lake,
Asleep in moonlight, or awake
To catch the color of the sky,
That sifts through every cloud swept by,—
How beautiful ye are, in change
Of sultry haze and storm-light strange;
How dream-like rest ye on the bar
That parts the billow from the star;
How blend your mists with waters clear,
Till earth floats off, and heaven seems near.

Ye faint and fade, a pearly zone,
The coast-line of a land unknown.
Yet that is sunburnt Ossipee,
Plunged knee-deep in the limpid sea:
Somewhere among these grouping isles,
Old White-Face from his cloud-cap smiles,
And gray Chocorua bends his crown,
To look on happy hamlets down;
And every pass and mountain-slope
Leads out and on some human hope.

Here, the great hollows of the hills,
The glamour of the June day fills.
Along the climbing path, the brier,
In rose-bloom beauty beckoning higher,
Breathes sweetly the warm uplands over;
And, gay with buttercups and clover,
The slopes of meadowy freshness make
A green foil to the sparkling lake.

So is it with yon hills that swim
Upon the horizon, blue and dim:
For all the summer is not ours;
On other shores familiar flowers
Find blossoming as fresh as these,
In shade and shine and eddying breeze;
And scented slopes as cool and green,
To kiss of lisping ripples lean.

So is it with the land beyond
This earth we press with step so fond.
Upon those faintly-outlined hills
God's sunshine sleeps, His dew distils:
The dear beatitudes of home
Within the heavenly boundaries come:
The hearts that made life's fragrance here

To Eden-haunts bring added cheer;
And all the beauty, all the good,
Lost to our lower altitude,
Transfigured, yet the same, are given,
Upon the mountain-heights of heaven.

O cloud-swathed hills the flood across,
Ye hide the mystery of our loss,
Yet hide it but a little while:
Past sunlit shore and shadowy isle,
Out to the still Lake's farther brim,
Erelong our bark the wave shall skim.
And what the vigor and the glow
Our earthly-torpid souls shall know,
When, grounding on the silver sands,
We feel the clasp of loving hands,
And see the walls of sapphire gleam,
Nor tongue can tell, nor heart can dream.

But in your rifts of wondrous light
Wherewith these lower fields are bright,
In every strengthening breeze that brings
The mountain-health upon its wings,
We own the gift of Pentecost,
And not one hint of heaven is lost.

CHILD AND WOMAN.

LITTLE NANNIE.

FAWN-footed Nannie,
  Where have you been?
"Chasing the sunbeams
  Into the glen;
Plunging through silver lakes
  After the moon;
Tracking o'er meadows
  The footsteps of June."

Sunny-eyed Nannie,
  What did you see?
"Saw the fays sewing
  Green leaves on a tree;
Saw the waves counting
  The eyes of the stars;
Saw cloud-lambs sleeping
  By sunset's red bars."

Listening Nannie,
  What did you hear?
"Heard the rain asking
  A rose to appear;
Heard the woods tell
  When the wind whistled wrong;
Heard the stream flow
  Where the bird drinks his song."

Nannie, dear Nannie,
  O take me with you,
To run and to listen,
  And see as you do!
"Nay, nay! you must borrow
  My ear and my eye,
Or the beauty will vanish,
  The music will die."

SWINGING IN THE BARN.

SWING away,
From the great cross-beam,
Hid in heaps of clover-hay,
Scented like a dream.

Higher yet!
Up, between the eaves,
Where the gray doves cooing flit
Through the sun-gilt leaves.

Here we go!
Whistle, merry wind!
'T is a long day you must blow,
Lighter hearts to find.

Swing away!
Sweep the rough barn floor;
Looking through on Arcady
Framed in by the door!

One, two, three!
Quick! the round red sun,
Hid behind yon twisted tree,
Means to end the fun.

Swing away,
Over husks and grain!
Shall we ever be as gay,
If we swing again?

WATCHING THE SNOW.

O SNOW! flying hither,
And hurrying thither,
Here, there, through the air,—you never care whither,—
Do you see me here sitting,
A-knitting, a-knitting,
And wishing myself with you breezily flitting,
Like any wild elf?

Lo! light as a feather,
The merry flakes gather
In rifts and in drifts, glad enough of cold weather;
Gay throngs interlacing,
On the slant roofs embracing,
They slip and they fall! down, down they are racing,
I after them all!

One large flake advances;
'T is a white steed that prances;
At the bits as he flits, how he foams, like my fancies!

Up softly I sidle
From where I sit idle, —
I snatch, as it flies, at the gossamer bridle, —
I am mounted, I rise!

Away we are bounding,
No hoof-note resounding,
Still as light is our flight through the armies surrounding;
No murmur, no rustling,
Though millions are jostling;
A host is in camp, but you heard neither bustling
Nor bugle, nor tramp.

Yet the truce-flag is lifted;
Unfurled it lies drifted
Over hill, over rill, where its snow could be sifted;
And now I'm returning
To parley concerning
The beautiful cause that awakened my yearning, —
The trouble that was.

Ho! ho! a swift fairy, —
A pearl-shallop airy!
I am caught, quick as thought! fleece-muffled and hairy,

Her grim boatman tightens
His rough grasp, and frightens
Me sore, as we sail to the east, where it lightens
On waves of the gale.

White, dimpled, and winning,
The fairy sits spinning,
From her hair, floating fair, coils of cable beginni
Her shallop to tether
In stress of bleak weather,
While the boatman and I, wrapped in ermine together
Drift on through the sky.

Stay! the boat is upsetting!
My fairy, forgetting
Her coil and her toil, to escape from a wetting,
Has now the one notion:
Below boils the ocean!
I scream, — I am heard, — up, in arrowy motion,
I am borne by a bird; —

A gray eagle! — over
The seas flies the rover;
And I ride as his guide, a new world to discover.

He bears me on, steady,
Through whirlwind and eddy;
I cling to his neck, and he ever is ready
To pause at my beck.

White doves through the ether
Come flocking together:
How they crowd to me, proud if I smooth one soft feather!
O what is the matter?
They startle, — they scatter!
On the wet window-pane hear my eagle's claws clatter! —
The snow's turned to rain!

PRUDENCE.

WHAT is this round world to Prudence,
  With her round, black, restless eyes,
But a world for knitting stockings,
  Sweeping floors, and baking pies?

'T is a world that women work in,
  Sewing long seams, stitch by stitch:
Barns for hay, and chests for linen; —
  'T is a world where men grow rich.

Ten years old is little Prudence;
  Ten years older still she seems,
With her busy eyes and fingers,
  With her grown-up thoughts and schemes.

Sunset is the time for candles;
  Cows are milked at fall of dew;
Beans will grow, and melons ripen,
  When the summer skies are blue.

Is there more than work in living?
  Yes; a child must go to school,
And to meeting every Sunday;
  Not a heathen be, or fool.

Something more has haunted Prudence
  In the song of bird and bee,
In the low wind's dreamy whisper
  Through the light-leaved poplar-tree.

Something lingers, bends above her,
  Leaning at the mossy well;
Some sweet murmur from the meadows;
  On the air some gentle spell.

But she will not stop to listen:—
  Maybe there are witches yet!
So she runs away from beauty;
  Tries its presence to forget.

'T is the way her mother taught her;
  Prudence is not much to blame.
Work is good for child or woman;
  Childhood's jailer,—'t is a shame!

Gravely at the romping children
  Their gray heads the gossips shake;
Saying, with a smile for Prudence,
  "What a good wife she will make!"

BLUE-EYED GRACE.

YOUR walk is lonely, blue-eyed Grace,
  Down the long forest-road to school,
Where shadows troop, at dismal pace,
  From sullen chasm to sunless pool.
Are you not often, little maid,
Beneath the sighing trees afraid?

"Afraid! beneath the tall, strong trees
  That bend their arms to shelter me,
And whisper down, with dew and breeze,
  Sweet sounds that float on lovingly,
Till every gorge and cavern seems
Thrilled through and through with fairy dreams?

"Afraid,—beside the water dim,
  That holds the baby lilies white
Upon its bosom, where a hymn
  Ripples forth softly to the light
That now and then comes gliding in,
A lily's budding smile to win?

"Fast to the slippery precipice
  I see the nodding harebell cling:
In that blue eye no fear there is;
  Its hold is firm, — the frail, free thing!
The harebell's Guardian cares for me,
So I am in safe company.

"The woodbine clambers up the cliff,
  And seems to murmur, 'Little Grace,
The sunshine were less welcome, if
  It brought not every day your face.'
Red leaves slip down from maples high,
And touch my cheek as they flit by.

"I feel at home with everything
  That has its dwelling in the wood;
With flowers that laugh, and birds that sing;
  Companions beautiful and good,
Brothers and sisters everywhere;
And over all our Father's care.

"In rose-time or in berry-time;
  When ripe seeds fall, or buds peep out;

When green the turf, or white the rime,
  There 's something to be glad about.
It makes my heart bound just to pass
The sunbeams dancing on the grass.

"And when the bare rocks shut me in
  Where not a blade of grass will grow,
My happy fancies soon begin
  To warble music rich and low,
And paint what eyes could never see:
My thoughts are company for me.

"What does it mean to be alone?
  And how is any one afraid
Who feels the dear God on his throne,
  Sending his sunshine through the shade,
Warming the damp sod into bloom,
And smiling off the thicket's gloom?

"At morning, down the woodpath cool,
  The fluttering leaves make cheerful talk.
After the stifled day at school,
  I hear, along my homeward walk,

The airy wisdom of the wood,
Far easiest to be understood!

"I whisper to the winds; I kiss
  The rough old oak, and clasp his bark;
No farewell of the thrush I miss;
  I lift the soft veil of the dark,
And say to bird, and breeze, and tree,
'Good night! good friends you are to me!'"

ROCK AND RILL.

"INTO the sunshine out of shade!"
The rill has heard the call,
And, babbling low, her answer made,—
A laugh, 'twixt slip and fall.

Out from her cradle-roof of trees,
Over the free, rough ground!
The peaceful blue above she sees;
The cheerful green around.

A pleasant world for running streams
To steal unnoticed through,
At play with all the sweet sky-gleams,
And nothing else to do!

A rock has stopped the silent rill,
And taught her how to speak:
He hinders her; she chides him still;
He loves her lispings weak.

And still he will not let her go:
  But she may chide and sing,
And o'er him liquid freshness throw,
  Amid her murmuring.

The harebell sees herself no more
  In waters clear at play;
Yet never she such azure wore,
  Till wept on by the spray.

And many a woodland violet
  Stays charmed upon the bank;
Her thoughtful blue eye brimming wet,
  The rock and rill to thank.

The rill is blessing in her talk
  What half she held a wrong,—
The happy trouble of the rock
  That makes her life a song.

IN THE RAIN.

A LIGHT flashed up in her sad blue eye,
Like a ray through a break in the cloudy sky,
As she leaned at the showered pane.
"Thank Heaven! he's come!"—but the train shrieked "Nay!"
And crashed o'er her dying hopes away.
Still she waited on till the day was gone,
Waited alone in the rain.

Ever, now and again, the cloud-rack through
There peeped a bud of the heavenly blue,—
Blue, without speck or stain.
Then the young corn shook in its jewelled mist,
And the violets twinkled, pure amethyst;
And her eye grew bright with a dewy light,
Waiting alone in the rain.

But the soft blue flower of the sky shut up
Behind the tempest its hollow cup;
The meadows were dim again:

And the warm light faded out of her eyes,
While she paced, and gazed on the restless skies,
  While she tried to keep her wild heart asleep,
    Waiting alone in the rain.

It streamed and poured from the shelving bank,
It sprinkled mire on the sedges rank;
    It beat on the springing grain.
"Come home!" called the horn from behind the hill:
She heard, but she lingered and listened still,
  Still, gazing back down the iron track,
    Waited alone in the rain.

The hours dragged by; it was dark and late;
The cars rushed on with their throbbing freight,
    Screaming a laugh at her pain.
But the west uncurtained a wide, clear space,
And the sunset lighted a laggard face,
  And the wild, wet day stole in smiles away,
    While two hurried home in the rain.

THE SCHOOLMISTRESS.

"HOW are you so cheerful,
  Gentle Edith Lane!
Be it bright or cloudy,
  Fall of dew or rain,
In that lonely schoolhouse,
  Patiently you stay,
Teaching simple children,
  All the livelong day."

"Teaching simple children?
  I am simple, too:
So we learn together
  Lessons plain as true,
From this thumb-worn Bible,
  Full of love's best lore;
Or, to read another,
  Just unlatch the door.

"Can I but be cheerful
While I bid them look,
Through the sunny pages
Of each opening book?—
Showing tracks of angels,
On the footworn sod;
Listening to the music
Nature makes to God."

"Have you then no sorrow,
Smiling Edith Lane?
Where the barberry's coral
Rattles on the pane,
Where, in endless yellow,
Autumn flowers I see,
Working for a living
Were a woe to me."

"Sorrow! I—a woman,
And in years not young?
Of the common chalice,
Drops are on my tongue.
What of that? No whisper
To my heart is lost,

From the barberry-clusters,
  Sweetened by the frost;

"From the rooted sunshine,—
  Golden-rod in bloom,
Lighting up the hillsides,
  For November's gloom.
Shall I blot with weeping
  Nature's joy and grace?
Rather be her gladness
  Mirrored in my face.

"'Working for a living'?
  May no worse befall!
Love is always busy;
  God works, over all.
Life is worth the earning,
  For its daily cheer,
Shared with those who love me,
  In yon cottage dear.

"If you can, fair lady,
  Go and be a drone!

Leave me with the children,
  Dear as if my own.
Leave me to the humming
  Of my little hive,
Glad to earn a living,
  Glad to be alive!"

GETTING ALONG.

WE trudge on together, my good man and I,
Our steps growing slow as the years hasten by,
Our children are healthy, our neighbors are kind,
And with the world round us we 've no fault to find,

'T is true that he sometimes will choose the worst way
For sore feet to walk in, a weary hot day;
But then my wise husband can scarcely go wrong
And, somehow or other, we 're getting along.

There are soft summer shadows beneath our home
trees:
How handsome he looks, sitting there at his ease!
We watch the flocks coming while sunset grows dim,
His thoughts on the cattle, and mine upon him.

The blackbirds and thrushes come chattering near;
I love the thieves' music, but listen with fear:

He shoots the gay rogues I would pay for their
song ; —
We 're different, sure ; still, we 're getting along.

He seems not to know what I eat, drink, or wear ;
He 's trim and he 's hearty, so why should I care ?
No harsh word from him my poor heart ever shocks :
I would n't mind scolding, — so seldom he talks.

Ah, well ! 't is too much that we women expect :
He only has promised to love and protect.
See, I lean on my husband, so silent and strong ;
I 'm sure there 's no trouble ; — we 're getting
along.

Life is n't so bright as it was long ago,
When he visited me amid tempest and snow ;
And would bring me a ribbon or jewel to wear,
And sometimes a rosebud to twist in my hair :

But when we are girls, we can all laugh and sing ;
Of course, growing old, life 's a different thing ;
My good man and I have forgot our May song,
But still we are quietly getting along.

'T is true I was rich; I had treasures and land;
But all that he asked was my heart and my hand:
Though people do say it, 't is what they can't prove, —
"He married for money; she, — poor thing! for
love."

My fortune is his, and he saves me its care;
To make his home cheerful 's enough for my share.
He seems always happy our broad fields among;
And so I 'm contented: — we 're getting along.

With stocks to look after, investments to find,
It's not very strange that I'm seldom in mind:
He can't stop to see how my time 's dragging on, —
And oh! *would* he miss me, if I should be gone?

Should he be called first, I must follow him fast,
For all that's worth living for then will be past.
But I 'll not think of losing him; fretting is wrong,
While we are so pleasantly getting along.

UNWEDDED.

BEHOLD her there in the evening sun,
That kindles the Indian Summer trees
To a separate burning bush, one by one,
Wherein the Glory Divine she sees!

Mate and nestlings she never had:
Kith and kindred have passed away;
Yet the sunset is not more gently glad,
That follows her shadow, and fain would stay.

For out of her life goes a breath of bliss,
And a sunlike charm from her cheerful eye,
That the cloud and the loitering breeze would miss;
A balm that refreshes the passer-by.

"Did she choose it, this single life?"
Gossip, she saith not, and who can tell?
But many a mother, and many a wife,
Draws a lot more lonely, we all know well.

Doubtless she had her romantic dream,
  Like other maidens, in May-time sweet,
That flushes the air with a lingering gleam,
  And goldens the grass beneath her feet: —

A dream unmoulded to visible form,
  That keeps the world rosy with mists of youth,
And holds her in loyalty close and warm,
  To her fine ideal of manly truth.

"But is she happy, a woman, alone?"
  Gossip, alone in this crowded earth,
With a voice to quiet its hourly moan,
  And a smile to heighten its rarer mirth?

There are ends more worthy than happiness:
  Who seeks it, is digging joy's grave, we know.
The blessed are they who but live to bless;
  She found out that mystery, long ago.

To her motherly, sheltering atmosphere,
  The children hasten from icy homes:
The outcast is welcome to share her cheer;
  And the saint with a fervent benison comes.

For the heart of woman is large as man's;
  God gave her his orphaned world to hold,
And whispered through her His deeper plans
  To save it alive from the outer cold.

And here is a woman who understood
  Herself, her work, and God's will with her,
To gather and scatter His sheaves of good,
  And was meekly thankful, though men demur.

Would she have walked more nobly, think,
  With a man beside her, to point the way,
Hand joining hand in the marriage-link?
  Possibly, Yes: it is likelier, Nay.

For all men have not wisdom and might:
  Love's eyes are tender, and blur the map;
And a wife will follow by faith, not sight,
  In the chosen footprint, at any hap.

In the comfort of home who is gladder than she?
  Yet, stirred by no murmur of "might have been,"
Her heart as a carolling bird soars free,
  With the song of each nest she has glanced within.

Having the whole, she covets no part:
  Hers is the bliss of all blessed things.
The tears that unto her eyelids start,
  Are those which a generous pity brings;

Or the sympathy of heroic faith
  With a holy purpose, achieved or lost.
To stifle the truth is to stop her breath,
  For she rates a lie at its deadly cost.

Her friends are good women and faithful men,
  Who seek for the True, and uphold the Right;
And who shall proclaim her the weaker, when
  Her very presence puts sin to flight?

"And dreads she never the coming years?"
  Gossip, what are the years to her?
All winds are fair, and the harbor nears,
  And every breeze a delight will stir.

Transfigured under the sunset trees,
  That wreathe her with shadowy gold and red,
She looks away to the purple seas,
  Whereon her shallop will soon be sped.

She reads the hereafter by the here:
  A beautiful Now, and a better To Be:
In life is all sweetness, in death no fear.—
  You waste your pity on such as she.

CHRIEMHILD.

YOU know the strange old Nibelungen story,
The fitful, billowy song of love and hate,—
Of rare Chriemhild, and her rose-garden's glory
By wrath laid desolate?

Glad shines that garden, with its leagues of roses,
Midway the old time and the new between;
Yet not a flower its silken bar encloses,
So sweet as the Rose-Queen.

She walks there in the young world's radiant morning,
Intwining hero-garlands, redly gay,
For her twelve knights, who, armed for battle-warning,
To watch the garden stay.

She seeks, undaunted, its remotest edges,
Cut from the forest's still and murky gloom,
Where, right against weird glens and caverned ledges,
The freshest roses bloom.

Black shadows, in behind the beech-leaves hidden,
That lean to clutch the sunshine's falling gold,
And dim, deep thickets, by white glimmerings thridden,
Send her no thrill of cold.

And she can hear, by woman's fears unshaken,
The warrior pine's long requiem on the air,
And winds astray, that from lone hollows waken
A wail, as of despair.

She can pluck roses, unaware of danger,
Since innocence keeps watch and ward within:
To evil dreads a careless, happy stranger,
Unvisited of sin.

One night a dream alighted in her bower:
A mystic falcon perched upon her hand;
Daring and beautiful, he curbed his power,
As waiting her command.

Then two fierce eagles through the azure swooping,
Plunged into that brave bird their cruel claws,
And snatched him from her sight, with sorrow drooping;
Ah! bitter was the cause!

For Siegfried was that falcon, her heart's chosen,
Though yet in maiden thought forsworn unseen.
An honored wife, — a widow horror-frozen, —
So reads thy fate, sweet queen.

Sweet queen! alas, alas! sweet queen no longer:
In fury and in anguish ends the dream;
The lurid lines of destiny burn stronger,
And hide her beauty's beam.

Gaze long upon the dear, sad face before you,
For never lovelier ladye will you see
In dew, and balm, and freshness bending o'er you, —
The Rose of Burgundy.

'T is on the wall of a Bavarian palace;[1]
A fresco by a master-limner wrought;
You see Chriemhild herself, ere wasting malice
Had all to ruin brought.

She clings to Siegfried, holding on her finger,
The falcon of her vision, — ominous bird!
While far off, where her chieftain's glances linger,
The rush of doom is heard.

Behold the nucleus of the old song's glory.
  This is the picture of Chriemhild to keep;
For you can only finish the mad story,
    To shudder and to weep.

Link not her name with Etzel's barbarous splendor,
  Nor the bold Nibelung race she snared to death:
Embalm her memory, womanly and tender,
    In love's most sacred breath!

You happier women of these later ages,
  With white hands by her hideous guilt unsoiled,—
Had she read forward her own history's pages,
    Like you she had recoiled.

Who hears, in that young, rapturous inspiration,
  When every thought takes up its harp and sings,
The undertone of demon-visitation
    Muttering beneath Love's wings?

Mean jealousies her queenly bosom fluttered,
  Wakening to war the monstrous brood of crime,
Dragon with fiend, until her tale is uttered,
    A fear unto all time.

Nay; end it with this portrait of a woman,
  To whom is possible yet a perfect lot.
When beauty once has blossomed in the human,
        Its blight remember not.

Even blotted so, her story is immortal.
  Transfigured by her love, Chriemhild shall stand,
Alway with Siegfried at the palace-portal,
        The dream-bird on her hand.

LEGEND OF A VEIL.[2]

SEVEN hundred years ago, a pair on whom
The accidental honor of a crown
Had worthily fallen, in their morning hour
Of bridal bliss, stood hand in hand, and gazed
Into a world which love makes Eden still;
Leopold of Austria and his Swabian bride.
The old baronial rampart where they stood
Frowned down upon Vienna, that smiled back.
They, in the open balcony of oak,
Sunlit and airy, saw the wide earth bloom
Around them like one flower, as lovers will:
And, for a while, they silently were glad.
Then, out of his full joy, young Leopold spoke:

"Beloved, see this beauteous realm of mine,
Whereof thou reignest queen. How all things smile
To welcome thy sweet looks! How every herb
And bough and thicket upward sends to thee
A pleasant smell! And He is surely pleased,

Who sits above the sun, and makes the world
Blossom with gladness, — He is surely pleased
To see us stand here happy in His sight.
Yet not even love brings satisfying bliss:
No joy that overflows must run to waste.
And work awaits us in this Paradise, —
Where thou shalt be my helpmeet; thou, mine Eve!
Rulers are gardeners only. Thou and I
Will toil among the earth-bedraggled vines
And frost-nipped blossoms of humanity,
Till life around looks fresh as Nature does,
Sunned in our love, and in the smile of God.

"Before I saw thy face, the mother of Christ
Was ever as a light amid my thoughts,
Charming me forth unto heroic deeds;
Showing the way of lowly sacrifice
Where kingly souls with her dear Son must walk.
My Agnes, from thy gentle eye distils
A ray more luminous in its tenderness
Through every inmost channel of resolve.
Thy woman's soul with my man's mind shall blend,

One work, one inspiration: I shall rule
Nobly through thee, my bride, my beautiful!"

As one who tunes a flute among the hills,
And hears, entranced, the music eddying back
In palpitating echoes through the air,
All unaware that he awoke that joy,
Agnes took softly up her husband's word
In charmed unconsciousness:
"O beautiful life,
O beautiful world, wherein I live with thee!
Thanks unto God, who made thee first my friend,
Then lover and husband. Little would it be
To stand beside thee here, thy wife and queen,
Were I not raised to nobler eminence,
Lifted to share with thee both work and thought,
Mate of thine aspirations. Friend, best friend,
And dearest always by that name to me,
Because the name is an immortal one, —
Might I not look as now in thy soul's eyes,
And feel thy love through larger and through less,
Diffusing calm, opening new wells of joy
That rise beyond expression, making all
I share with thee as sacramental food,

What had been left? The thought is bitter bleak:
Dreary and gray as the Siberian wilds,
Had spread my life. But God would still have been:
I should have met him in the wilderness,
Thee, afterward, perhaps, in Heaven.
                                        Mine own!
Whene'er I hear the convent vesper-bell,
Or echo of a midnight cloister-chant,
The manly chorals in sonorous praise
Responding to the unseen sisters' hymn,
I think there may be hearts like thine and mine,
Hidden behind the nun's veil and the cowl,
Forever separated, yet so near!
God listens through the screens they cannot lift;
The chords lost here ring full in heaven. And yet
'T is surely better to strike all the keys
Of this our manifold being to His praise,
Sending through low and high, through discords even,
One thrill of unison. All we have is His,
And we ourselves; and we will live so here,
That in that land where are no marriages,
We shall forever in one mansion dwell,
Still finding Heaven in some joint work for Him.

Ah, what can Heaven be, and this earth so fair?
River that waterest Eden, art thou then
More glorious than our Danube, when the doors
Of the East are open, and the sunshine pours
Upon his path between the solemn hills,
And over the green, grateful fields? And thou,
City of Light, aglow with jasper walls
And gates of pearl, art thou more beautiful
Than our Vienna, lifting up her hands
To us from cottage-lattice, tower, and spire,
Beckoning from her innumerable lives
That we can bless, and shall?
O royal life,
Royal to all who carry royal hearts,
Thou shalt be benediction to our realm!
Let us build tabernacles here, beloved,
On durable foundations of deep bliss.
Upon some height let us set up a house,
A home for holy men, to sanctify
The memory of this, our marriage-day."

So spake that happy bride, and upward looked
To meet the answer of her husband's eyes.
Bending, he lifted her white, floating veil,

And touched her forehead with his lips, and said
With reverent earnestness, "We will."
The wind,
The only listener passing, heard their vow,
And suddenly and lightly took the veil
And bore it far along the orange-boughs,
And over the rose-gardens all in bloom,
And hid it in the green woods out of sight.

Then Leopold sent out squires to bring it back,
For Agnes' sake, who could not bear to lose
One token of their married happiness;
But none could find it. And the cheerful years
Passed over them like days, filled to the brim
With princely undertakings, and perfumed
With gratitude, which every princely heart
Takes as a spur to steadier energy,
And fervor of well-doing: so the vow
Of that fair morning from their memory passed

Years after, as a summer twilight fell,
Giving his flagging steed a languid rein,
Duke Leopold let his huntsmen homeward ride
Far out of sight before him. Through a glen

He loitered on, where never hoof had trod,
Crushing the juicy bracken and crisp turf,
All spray, and spice, and coolness; under pines
That lifted their green tops like minster-spires
Into blue light above, and hid their ranks
Of spectral stems and dimly-woven boughs
In deeper than cathedral gloom behind.
Out of the wood a silent rivulet stole,
And caught the red of sunset, and then crept
Into the shadow of the beckoning ferns.
A bird trilled from a bush: within the wood
Another answered; then a hundred sang.
The shivering sweetness through the bracken passed,
And Leopold halted. Standing by his steed,
Against the darkened forest, with the glow
Of sunset falling on his upturned brow,
Strange peace enthralled him; and subdued he said,
"This is a holy place, a holy hour:
Here might the angels walk."
Even while he spoke,
He caught a glimpse of wavering whiteness swayed
Within a dingle close at hand. Thereat
Startled one moment, instincts of a knight
In the next spurred him towards the mystery,

And lo, the veil of Agnes! It had hung
Here, in the sanctuary of the wood,
Heaven-kept, while robber-tempests went and came,
With the birds singing round it, and the flowers
Filling it with perfume, from spring to spring,
In token of a promise unfulfilled.
Leopold was touched. Yet, thridding a blind path
Out of the glimmering twilight of the pines,
"Ever," he said, "I doubted if the monks
Praised God so well as many an honest serf,
Who earned his bread and ate it thankfully.
They pitch their notes too high for humble folk,
And call the common singing sacrilege.
If peasants thank our Lord for anything,
It is for wife, and little ones, and home,
As I for my sweet Agnes and her babes.
No saintly joy is this, the brethren say,
And pity us and pray for us, and wrap
Themselves in cloaks of sanctity, and walk
Their shining road to heaven above our heads,--
Pavement of gold that we must keep repaired,
Whate'er befalls us in the thoroughfare,
Or on the broken bridge across the chasm.
Labor, methinks, and prayer are of one piece.

Nay, toil is also praise, the best, from those
Whose fingers are more flexile than their tongues.

"Alack! what do I murmur to myself?
Agnes would grieve to overhear these thoughts.
She likens prayers and hymns unto a stream
Flowing amid the sandy wastes of life,
Watering the roots of action; nerving up
The earnest toiler's strength; the wine of heaven.
Our priests sit at the guarded fountain-head,
To keep the waters pure, and pour the wine
For fainting pilgrims. Niggardly it were,
Saith she, to grudge them shelter, who prepare
A tent for us amid the wilderness.
And Agnes is to me what all these hymns
And chants and mighty chorals are to her,—
A glorious lifting-up; to heart, delight;
To hands, unbounded strength. I would I were
A good King Robert[3] for her sake, to vein
The court and camp with rills of saintly song,
A thrill of *Veni Sancte Spiritus*
To waken underneath the satin scarfs
And ermine mantles of my followers.
I am but Leopold, an ungifted man,

Save for my ducal crown and her dear love.
A vow is still a vow, though tardily kept.
She shall behold a stately cloister built
Within the glen that hid her bridal veil.
And I will toil on, hoping yet to see
Each hut within my realm a home like mine,
And every peasant happy as a duke."

So Kloster-Neuberg rose among the hills;
There Agnes' veil is shrined, and Leopold there
Is worshipped as a saint.
Good man, he sleeps
Too soundly to be vexed by anything
That may be said or sung above his grave.
Perhaps he would have thought the monks misplaced
The aureole that they set upon his brow,
Not on his bride's. No doubt he would have asked
To be remembered for some other work
Than convent-building: but he could not choose;
He is a saint perforce. The healthier grace
Of honorable manhood counts him naught,
And less than naught his household happiness:
Within the threshold laid by wedded joy,
The very thought of it is sacrilege.

And yet the buried sweetness of true love
That once hung rose-wreaths round the Austrian
throne,
The brethren with a deprecating sigh
Will sometimes air, unfolding Agnes' veil.

FROM WITHOUT.

ENTANGLED.

BIRDS among the budding trees,
  Blossoms on the ringing ground:
Light from those? or song from these?
  Can the tangle be unwound?

For the bluebird's warbled note,
  Violet-odors hither flung;
And the violet curved her throat,
  Just as if she sat and sung.

Dandelions dressed in gold,
  Give out echoes clear and loud,
To the oriole's story, told
  With gay poise and gesture proud.

And the swaying yellow-bird,
  Trilling, thrills their hollow stems,

Until every root is stirred,
  Under their dropped diadems.

Swallows thicken through the air, —
  Curve and drift of plumy brown, —
Wafting, showering everywhere,
  Melody's light seed-notes down.

Beauty, music on the earth;
  Music, beauty in the sky;
Guess the mystery of their birth!
  All the haunting what and why.

Nature weaves a marvellous braid;
  Tints and tones how deftly blent.
Who unwinds the web she made?
  Thou, who wearest her wise content.

Wrapped within her beauty's fold,
  Of her song thyself a part,
Plainly are her secrets told
  Unto thee, O pure of heart!

THE RIDDLE OF BEAUTY.

BROWN bird of spring, on pinion soft
Ascending,
A voice to reddening dawn aloft
Thus lending;
Few heed thy song; why is it sweet?
Why art thou beautiful as fleet,
Light comer,
Bewildered in the stir and heat
Of summer?

White clouds, that over the blue sky
Are pressing,
The pilots of an argosy
Of blessing;
Ye float with all your sails unfurled
Above a dull, unconscious world;
None caring
Whence ye those fleeces, golden-curled,
Are bearing.

Blue autumn flower, thy deep heart stores
Heaven's azure;
And thence from out thy chalice pours
Rare pleasure.
The frost a plague-spot blackening casts;
Thy fringe is torn when sleety blasts
Grow stronger;
Men love thee while thy beauty lasts;
No longer.

Thou maid, around whose lip and eye
Intwining,
The loveliest tints of earth and sky
Are shining, —
Thy sweet song dies; thy freshness must
Fade like a flower's, by blight and dust
O'ertaken;
And all the roots of mortal trust
Are shaken.

O, why should thus the beautiful
O'erbrood us,
Yet ever its harmonious rule
Elude us?

The grave its hopeless blot may be;
Largess to eyes that cannot see
'T is giving:
The joy, the pain, the mystery
Of living.

Say whence, O Beauty, floatest thou,
And whither?
But in a shade, an echo now
Swept hither.
Born with the sounds that hurry past?
Dead with the shapes that flee so fast?
O, never!
The soul of each fair thing must last
Forever.

The glory of the rose remains
Unfaded,
Though now no wreath from blossoming lanes
Be braided.
A word unknown she drooping said;
A breath was in her, from the dead
To waft her:
And Beauty's riddle shall be read
Hereafter.

HINTS.

SWEET Nature, speak to me!
I have been listening so long, so long!
The goldfinch round the linden winds his song:
A spangled butterfly just flew this way,
And stopped, as if he had some word to say;
The water-lily's leaves are half apart,
Pale with some secret hidden in her heart.
I hear, but yet the inner sense is sealed;
For me there is a mystery unrevealed:
Sweet Nature, speak to me!

Dear Book of Mystery,
Whose leaves a breeze of June is turning o'er,
To show me one forgotten word the more,
The living truths upon thy page are dry
As last year's violets that beside them lie:
The pastures green, the waters flowing still,
The shepherds' watch on Bethlehem's moonlit
hill,

Are but as tales of any common book:
Where is the light by which my soul should look,
Dear Book of Mystery?

Love is both eye and ear.
When like the west wind breathes my longing prayer,
Pausing the need of humblest hearts to share,
Then will sweet parables unfold their sense,
And Nature speak with all her eloquence.
Let the heart stagnate o'er its selfish dreams,
And life a veiled and silent statue seems:
Leaning upon the bosom of the Lord,
Love hears the lightest whisper of His word.
Love is both eye and ear.

The grace of the bending grasses,
The flush of the dawn-lit sky,
The scent that lingers and passes
When the loitering wind goes by,—
Are gushes and hints of sweetness,
From the unseen deeps afar;
The foam-edge of heaven's completeness
Swept outward through flower and star.

For the cloud, and the leaf, and the blossom,
  The shadow, the flickering beam,
Are waifs on the sea-like bosom
  Of beauty beyond our dream:
Its glow to our earth is given;
  It freshens this lower air:
O, the fathomless wells of heaven, —
  The springs of the earth rise there!

They whose hearts are whole and strong,
    Loving holiness,
Living clean from soil of wrong,
    Wearing truth's white dress, —
They unto no far-off height
    Wearily need climb;
Heaven to them is close in sight
    From these shores of time.

Only the anointed eye
    Sees in common things, —
Gleams dropped daily from the sky, —
    Heavenly blossomings.

To the hearts where light has birth
  Nothing can be drear;
Budding through the bloom of earth,
  Heaven is always near.

"Take the fruit I give you," says the bending tree;
"Nothing but a burden is it all to me.
Lighten ye my branches: let them toss in air!
Only leave me freedom next year's load to bear."

"Do my waters cheer thee," says the gurgling spring,
"With the crystal coolness 't is their life to bring?
Leave me not to stagnate, creeping o'er the plain;
Drink for thy refreshment; drink, and come again!"

"Can I yield you blessings?" says the friendly heart.
"Fear not I am poorer, though I much impart.
Wherefore should you thank me? giving is my need.
Love that wrought none comfort sorrow were indeed."

The curtain of the dark
  Is pierced by many a rent:
Out of the star-wells, spark on spark
  Trickles through night's torn tent.

Grief is a tattered tent
  Wherethrough God's light doth shine.
Who glances up, at every rent
  Shall catch a ray divine.

Thou mayst not rest in any lovely thing,
  Thou, who wert formed to seek and to aspire;
For no fulfilment of thy dreams can bring
  The answer to thy measureless desire.

The beauty of the round, green world is not
  Of the world's essence; far within the sky
The tints which make this bubble bright are wrought:
  The bubble bursts; the light can never die.

Thou canst not make a pillow for thy head
  Of anything so brittle and so frail;
Yet mayst thou by its transient glow be led
  Into the heaven where sun and star grow pale;

Where, out of burning whiteness, flows the light;
  Light, which is but the visible stream of love;—
Hope's ladder, brightening upward through the night,
  Whereon our feet grow winged as they move.

Let beauty sink in light; in central deeps
  Of love unseen, let dearest eyes grow dim:
They draw us after, up the infinite steeps
  Where souls familiar track the seraphim.

THE DEATH OF JUNE.

JUNE falls asleep upon her bier of flowers:
In vain are dewdrops sprinkled over her;
In vain would fond winds fan her back to life.
Her hours are numbered on the floral dial;
Astræa's scales have weighed her minutes out,
Poised on the Zodiac; and the Northern Crown
Hangs sparkling in the Zenith just at eve,
To show a queen is passing. See where stands,
Pausing on tiptoe, with full, flushing lips,
And outstretched arms, her sister, bright July,
Eager to kiss the blossoms, that will fade
If her hot breath but touch them.

June is dead.
Dead, without dread or pain, her gayest wreaths
Twined with her own hands for her funeral.
At first she smiled upon us, garlanded
With columbines and azure lupine-buds;
But now we find a few pale roses, dropped
In her last dreamy loitering through the fields,

Or see her wild geraniums by the brook;
Her laurels and azalias in the woods.
These gather we as keepsakes of dear June,
Though not unmindful of the humbler flowers
That thought it joy to bloom around her feet;—
The buttercups and blue-eyed-grass that peeped
Under the wayside bars at travellers;
Prunella lingering in the wagon's track;
The evening primrose, glimmering like a star
When the sun set; and the prim mullein too,
Folded in flannels from the eastern winds,
Damp dews, and reckless songs of bob-o'-links.

A warmer reign begins, and they must fade
Beneath its splendor; even these richer blooms,—
Orchis and Arethusa quaintly robed,
And harebells nodding to blue skies and streams,
And white pond-lilies, scarcely opening
In time to catch the farewell look of June:
But the midsummer air is balmy yet,
With the sweet, lingering breath of flowers that
died,
And left their fragrance for a legacy
To weary, dusty days they never saw.

Nature has meanings for the wise to guess.
The grass springs up like good thoughts in a soul
That loves and blesses all things, high and low.
The rose breathes out a passion and a beauty
Far sweeter than her bloom. And God sends man,
When he approaches heaven with lofty words,
To the green cloisters, where, from whitest calm,
The lily of the valley's incense-cloud
Ascends to Him like an unspoken prayer.
The universe is one great, loving thought,
Written in hieroglyphs of bud and bloom;
And we in human faces, human forms,
Not overgrown or ruinous with sin,
The same inspiring characters may read;
May feel sweet emanations from the life
Of one whose soul is closely knit with God's,
As if the gates of balmy Paradise
Again swung open to this outcast world.

Creator, Father! Thou art nature's wealth.
Suns, blossoms, insects, worlds, and souls of men,
Draw life's deep joy from Thee, their treasury.
Oft, like a beggar suddenly made rich,
I sink beneath the overpowering sense

Of Thee in all things. Sometimes 't is the moon,
Orbed like an Eye dilating with calm love,
That drowns me in pale, silent waves of light;
Sometimes it is the mighty, shadowing hills,
That crush me with a greatness not their own:
Or stars burn glory through me, living coals
On the heaped altar of the universe.

But whispers oftener, borne from common things,
Waken a subtle faculty within,
A sense of deeper beauty yet unbreathed:
As at the rainbow-bridge sat Asgard's ward
Listening through every season, and could hear
The grass grow leagues away, — so comes to me
A golden gladness, with keen, delicate edge
Piercing the films that wrap the inner sense,
Making it joy to think of swelling buds,
And fruit slow-ripening on the apple-trees,
And young birds fledging in the robin's nest:
By every outward sluice runs through my soul,
And overflows its brim, the thought of Thee!

But the swift memory of man and sin
Returns, and drains away my happiness.

H

O God! that man were good! That he would not
Make himself pestilent by brooding long
O'er evil thoughts and deeds, — a wind that lurks
For poisons in the marsh: — that he were true
And loving, like all natural things, that grow
Best in the sunshine, drawing from Thy light
Their joy, their strength from working Thy firm
will!
Then were this human life a summer breeze
Freshening the earth with balmy draughts of bloom;
And death were but subsiding into heaven,
As June flowers softly fade upon the light
Of brighter noons, yet leave their breath behind.

THE INDIAN SUMMER.

'TIS the time
When the chime
Of the seasons' choral band is ringing out
Smoky brightness fills the air,
For the light winds everywhere
Censers full of flowery embers swing about.
There is sweetness that oppresses,
As a tender parting blesses;
There's a softened glow of beauty,
As when Love is wreathing Duty;
There are melodies that seem
Weaving past and future into one fair dream

To her bier
Comes the year
Not with weeping and distress, as mortals do,
But, to guide her way to it,
All the trees have torches lit;
Blazing red the maples shine the woodlands through;

Gay witch-hazels in the river
Watch their own bright tapers quiver;
Flickering burn the birches yellow
Through the walnuts brown and mellow;
Dark, sad pines stand breathless by,
Mourners sole, and mourning that they cannot die.

Through the trees
Tolls the breeze.
Tolls, then rings a merry peal, and tolls again.
Dead leaves, shaken by the sound,
Slowly float and drop around.
So does memory lull or echo thoughts of pain.
Dead leaves lie upon earth's bosom,
Side by side with many a blossom;
Gentians, fringed with azure glory, —
Sky-flakes, dropped on meadows hoary;
Asters, thick and bright as sparks
Struck by seraph oarsmen from their starry barks

O, to die
When the sky
Smiles behind the Indian Summer's hazy veil!

Thus to glorify decay,
Going in life's best array,
Unto groves where death is a forgotten tale.
Falls a sorrow on the spirit?
Heavenly hopes are springing near it.
Earth, a happy child, rejoices,
Keeping time with angel voices.
When such autumn days are done,
There's a crown behind thy rays, thou setting sun!

WOULD YOU?

COULD you keep the tints of spring
  On the woods in misty brightness;
Keep the half-veiled boughs a-swing
  To the linnet's flitting lightness;
Through the birch leaves' rippling green
  Hold the maple-keys from dropping;
On the sward with May-showers clean,
  Cheat the violets into stopping;

Could you make the rosebud's lips
  Vow to be a bud forever;
From the sedges' wavering tips,
  Bid the pendent dewdrop never;
Could you make the sunrise hour
  For a lifetime overbrood you;
Could you change the year's full dower
  For its first faint promise,—would you?

Though joy beads the cup we quaff,
  Bubbling from the fount of morning,

When the world is all a laugh,
  And a welcome without warning;
At life's Cana-feast, the guest,
  Lingering on with thirst unsated,
Finds a later draught the best:
  Miracles, — when thou hast waited!

Thought must shade and sun the soul
  With its glorious mutations;
Every life-song is a whole
  Sweeter for its variations.
Wherefore with your bliss at strife?
  'T was an angel that withstood you.
Could you change your perfect life
  For a dream of living, — would you?

BETTER.

THAT haunting dream of Better,
  Forever at our side!
It tints the far horizon,
  It sparkles on the tide.
The cradle of the Present
  Too narrow is for rest:
The feet of the Immortal
  Leap forth to seek the Best.

O beauty, trailing sadness!
  Despair, hope's loftiest birth!
With tears and aspirations
  Have ye bedewed the earth.
The opening buds of April
  Untimely frost may chill;
The soul of sweet October
  Faints out in mystery still.

What buriest thou, gay childhood?
  Swift youth, what fled with thee?

Laugh'st at our losses, Sorrow,
As in some godlike glee?
Away, away forever
Our vessels seem to sail:
The Eternal Breath o'ertakes them;
Home speeds them every gale.

The filmy gold and purple
Swathed not the hills we trod:
'T was hard and common climbing,
The bramble and the clod.
The bitterness we tasted
Was Truth's most wholesome leaven:
The friends that left us lonely
Are opening doors in heaven.

And now the deeper midnight
Uncovers larger stars;
And grafts of glory bourgeon
From earthly blights and scars.
And now the mists are lifting —
The tides are rushing in —
'T is sunrise on the mountains! —
Lo! life is yet to win!

THE ROSE ENTHRONED.

IT melts and seethes, the chaos that shall grow
  To adamant beneath the house of life;
In hissing hatred atoms clash, and go
    To meet intenser strife.

And ere that fever leaves the granite veins,
  Down thunders over them a torrid sea:
Now Flood, now Fire, alternate despot reigns,
    Immortal foes to be.

Built by the warring elements, they rise,
  The massive earth-foundations, tier on tier,
Where slimy monsters with unhuman eyes
    Their hideous heads uprear.

The building of the world is not for you,
  That glare upon each other, and devour:
Race floating after race fades out of view,
    Till beauty springs from power.

Meanwhile from crumbling rocks and shoals of death
Shoots up rank verdure to the hidden sun;
The gulfs are eddying to the vague, sweet breath
Of richer life begun;

Richer and sweeter far than aught before,
Though rooted in the grave of what has been:
Unnumbered burials yet must heap Earth's floor
Ere she her heir shall win;

And ever nobler lives and deaths more grand,
For nourishment of that which is to come;
While mid the ruins of the work she planned
Sits Nature, blind and dumb.

For whom or what she plans, she knows no more
Than any mother of her unborn child:
Yet beautiful forewarnings murmur o'er
Her desolations wild.

Slowly the clamor and the clash subside;
Earth's restlessness her patient hopes subdue;
Mild oceans shoreward heave a pulse-like tide;
The skies are veined with blue.

And life works through the growing quietness,
  To bring some darling mystery into form:
Beauty her fairest Possible would dress
    In colors pure and warm.

Within the depths of palpitating seas
  A tender tint,—anon a line of grace,
Some lovely thought from its dull atom frees,
    The coming joy to trace:—

A pencilled moss on tablets of the sand,
  Such as shall veil the unbudded maiden-blush
Of beauty yet to gladden the green land;—
    A breathing, through the hush,

Of some sealed perfume longing to burst out,
  And give its prisoned rapture to the air;—
A brooding hope, a promise through a doubt,
    Is whispered everywhere.

And, every dawn a shade more clear, the skies
  A flush as from the heart of heaven disclose:
Through earth and sea and air a message flies,
    Prophetic of the Rose.

At last a morning comes, of sunshine still,
  When not a dewdrop trembles on the grass,
When all winds sleep, and every pool and rill
          Is like a burnished glass

Where a long looked-for guest might lean to gaze;
  When Day on Earth rests royally, — a crown
Of molten glory, flashing diamond rays,
          From heaven let lightly down.

In golden silence, breathless, all things stand;
  What answer waits this questioning repose?
A sudden gush of light and odors bland,
          And, lo, — the Rose! the Rose!

The birds break into canticles around;
  The winds lift Jubilate to the skies;
For, twin-born with the rose on Eden-ground,
          Love blooms in human eyes.

Life's marvellous queen-flower blossoms only so,
  In dust of low ideals rooted fast.
Ever the Beautiful is moulded slow
          From truth in errors past.

What fiery fields of Chaos must be won,
  What battling Titans rear themselves a tomb,
What births and resurrections greet the sun
      Before the rose can bloom!

And of some wonder-blossom yet we dream
  Whereof the time that is infolds the seed;
Some flower of light, to which the Rose shall seem
      A fair and fragile weed.

WAR-MEMORIES.

THE NINETEENTH OF APRIL.

[1861.]

THIS year, till late in April, the snow fell thick
and light:
Thy flag of truce, kind Nature, in clinging drifts of
white,
Hung over field and city: — now everywhere is
seen,
In place of that white quietness, a sudden glow of
green.

The verdure climbs the Common, beneath the leaf-
less trees,
To where the glorious Stars and Stripes are float-
ing on the breeze.
There, suddenly as Spring awoke from Winter's
snow-draped gloom,
The Passion-Flower of Seventy-Six is bursting into
bloom.

Dear is the time of roses, when earth to joy is
wed,
And garden-plat and meadow wear one generous
flush of red;
But now in dearer beauty, to her ancient colors true,
Blooms the old town of Boston in red and white and
blue.

Along the whole awakening North are those bright
emblems spread;
A summer noon of patriotism is burning overhead.
No party badges flaunting now, — no word of clique
or clan;
But "Up for God and Union!" is the shout of
every man.

O, peace is dear to Northern hearts; our hard-
earned homes more dear;
But Freedom is beyond the price of any earthly
cheer;
And Freedom's flag is sacred; — he who would
work it harm,
Let him, although a brother, beware our strong
right arm!

A brother! ah, the sorrow, the anguish of that word!
The fratricidal strife begun, when will its end be heard?
Not this the boon that patriot hearts have prayed and waited for; —
We loved them, and we longed for peace: but they would have it war.

Yes; war! on this memorial day, the day of Lexington,
A lightning-thrill along the wires from heart to heart has run.
Brave men we gazed on yesterday, to-day for us have bled:
Again is Massachusetts blood the first for freedom shed.

To war, — and with our brethren, then, — if only this can be!
Life hangs as nothing in the scale against dear Liberty!
Though hearts be torn asunder, for Freedom we will fight:
Our blood may seal the victory, but God will shield the Right!

THE SINKING OF THE MERRIMACK.

[MAY, 1862.]

GONE down in the flood, and gone out in the flame!
What else could she do, with her fair Northern name?
Her font was a river whose last drop is free:
That river ran boiling with wrath to the sea,
To hear of her baptismal blessing profaned,—
A name that was Freedom's, by treachery stained.

'T was the voice of our free Northern mountains that broke
In the sound of her guns, from her stout ribs of oak:
'T was the might of the free Northern hand you could feel
In her sweep and her moulding, from topmast to keel:

When they made her speak treason (does Hell know
of worse?)
How her strong timbers shook with the shame of
her curse!

Let her go! Should a deck so polluted again
Ever ring to the tread of our true Northern men?
Let the suicide-ship thunder forth, to the air
And the sea she has blotted, her groan of despair!
Let her last heat of anguish throb out into flame,
Then sink them together,—the ship and the name!

WEAVING.

ALL day she stands before her loom;
  The flying shuttles come and go:
By grassy fields, and trees in bloom,
  She sees the winding river flow.
And fancy's shuttle flieth wide,
And faster than the waters glide.

Is she entangled in her dreams,
  Like that fair weaver of Shalott,
Who left her mystic mirror's gleams,
  To gaze on light Sir Lancelot?
Her heart, a mirror sadly true,
Brings gloomier visions into view.

"I weave, and weave, the livelong day:
  The woof is strong, the warp is good:
I weave, to be my mother's stay;
  I weave, to win my daily food:
But ever as I weave," saith she,
"The world of women haunteth me.

"The river glides along, one thread
  In nature's mesh, so beautiful!
The stars are woven in; the red
  Of sunrise; and the rain-cloud dull.
Each seems a separate wonder wrought;
Each blends with some more wondrous thought.

"So, at the loom of life, we weave
  Our separate shreds, that varying fall,
Some stained, some fair; and, passing, leave
  To God the gathering up of all,
In that full pattern, wherein man
Works blindly out the eternal plan.

"In his vast work, for good or ill,
  The undone and the done he blends.
With whatsoever woof we fill,
  To our weak hands His might He lends,
And gives the threads beneath His eye
The texture of eternity.

"Wind on, by willow and by pine,
  Thou blue, untroubled Merrimack!

Afar, by sunnier streams than thine,
  My sisters toil, with foreheads black;
And water with their blood this root,
Whereof we gather bounteous fruit.

"There be sad women, sick and poor;
  And those who walk in garments soiled:
Their shame, their sorrow, I endure;
  By their defect my hope is foiled:
The blot they bear is on my name;
Who sins, and I am not to blame?

"And how much of your wrong is mine,
  Dark women slaving at the South?
Of your stolen grapes I quaff the wine;
  The bread you starve for fills my mouth:
The beam unwinds, but every thread
With blood of strangled souls is red.

"If this be so, we win and wear
  A Nessus-robe of poisoned cloth;
Or weave them shrouds they may not wear, —
  Fathers and brothers falling both

On ghastly, death-sown fields, that lie
Beneath the tearless Southern sky.

"Alas! the weft has lost its white.
It grows a hideous tapestry,
That pictures war's abhorrent sight:—
Unroll not, web of destiny!
Be the dark volume left unread,—
The tale untold,—the curse unsaid!"

So up and down before her loom
She paces on, and to and fro,
Till sunset fills the dusty room,
And makes the water redly glow,
As if the Merrimack's calm flood
Were changed into a stream of blood.

Too soon fulfilled, and all too true
The words she murmured as she wrought:
But, weary weaver, not to you
Alone was war's stern message brought:
"Woman!" it knelled from heart to heart,
"Thy sister's keeper know thou art!"

WAITING FOR NEWS.

[July 4, 1863.]

AT the corner of the lane,
Where we stood this time last year,
Droops and waves the ripening grain;
Sounds the meadow-lark's refrain,
Just as sad and clear.

Cornel-trees let blossoms fall
In a white shower at my feet;
Thick viburnums hide the wall;
And behind, the bush-bird's call
Bubbles, summery-sweet,

Now, as then, o'er purple blooms
Veiled by meadow-grasses rare;
Bubbles through the coppice glooms;
Joins the sweetbrier's late perfumes
Wandering through the air.

All returns ; — your word, your look,
  As we stood where now I stand : —
With a dread I could not brook,
Well I knew my faint voice shook,
    While you held my hand.

Firm you always were, and then
  High resolve had made you strong.
Could I bid you linger, when
Freedom called aloud for men
    To requite her wrong ?

Southrons threw their gauntlet-lie
  In the face of God and Truth.
"Go, for love's sake !" was my cry ;
"Were not Truth more dear than I,
    Thou wert naught, in sooth !"

And you went. The whole year through,
  I have felt war's thunder-quake
Rend me hour by hour anew :
Yet I would not call for you,
    Though my heart should break.

Only, standing here to-day,
  With the sweetbrier's wandering breath,
And the smell of new-mown hay
In the air, "This life," I say,
    "Strikes deep root in death."

Death! while here I pass the hours,
  Blood is rising round your feet:
I sit ankle-deep in flowers:
On you, red shot falls in showers,
    Through the battle-heat.

What if there I saw you lie,
  Where the grasses nod and blow,
With your forehead to the sky,
And your wounds — O God! that I, —
    That I bade you go!

Yet, were that to say once more,
  "Go," I'd say, "at any cost!"
Many a heart has bled before.
God his heroes will restore;
    No great soul is lost.

And the strife that rages so
  Burns out meanness from the land.
Men must fall, and blood must flow,
That our Plants of Honor grow
    Unto stature grand.

Ay, to-day it seems to me,
  That yon little straggling rose
Fed by War's red springs must be:
All of fair and good I see,
    Out of anguish grows.

Vines that shade the cottage-home;
  Laurels for the warrior's wreath;
Lilies of white peace, that bloom
After battle's lurid gloom; —
    All are nursed by death.

By our bond, I 'm close to-day
  As your sword is, to your side.
If your breath stops in the fray,
Watchers from above will say,
    Two for freedom died.

Still I loiter in the lane,—
  If I might but send you, dear,
Sweetbrier scents, the lark's refrain,
They would soothe the battle-pain;
  You should feel me near:

And the fresh thought of these fields
  With new strength would nerve your arm.
Fearlessly his sword he wields,
Whose whole risk is what it shields,—
    Home-love, pure and warm.

And you ventured this; you gave
  Freely all your wealth of life,
That the Stars and Stripes might wave
Nevermore above a slave.
    Cheerfully your wife

Climbs with you great Freedom's pyre,—
  Not as Hindoo widows die.
We to life in Life aspire:
Love's last height is our desire;
    Lo! we tread the sky!

Treading with a joyful scorn
  Selfish joy beneath our feet:
In a nation's hope new-born,
In a free world's radiant morn,
    Breathing bliss complete.

Hark! a jubilee of bells
  Pealing through the sunset light,
Shaking out fresh clover-smells!
Parting day to-morrow tells,
    Victory 's in sight.

Hark, again! the long, shrill blast
  Eager throngs are waiting for.
Is it Death's train, sweeping past?
Homeward, Heart! Pain cannot last.
    What news from the war?

A LOYAL WOMAN'S NO.

NO! is my answer from this cold, bleak ridge,
Down to your valley: you may rest you there
The gulf is wide, and none can build a bridge
That your gross weight would safely hither bear.

Pity me, if you will. I look at you
With something that is kinder far than scorn,
And think, "Ah, well! I might have grovelled, too;
I might have walked there, fettered and forsworn."

I am of nature weak as others are;
I might have chosen comfortable ways;
Once from these heights I shrank, beheld afar,
In the soft lap of quiet, easy days.

I might, — I will not hide it, — once I might
Have lost, in the warm whirlpools of your voice,
The sense of Evil, the stern cry of Right;
But Truth has steered me free, and I rejoice.

Not with the triumph that looks back to jeer
At the poor herd that call their misery bliss;
But as a mortal speaks when God is near,
I drop you down my answer: it is this:

am not yours, because you prize in me
What is the lowest in my own esteem:
Only my flowery levels can you see,
Nor of my heaven-smit summits do you dream.

am not yours, because you love yourself:
Your heart has scarcely room for me beside.
will not be shut in with name and pelf;
I spurn the shelter of your narrow pride!

Not yours, — because you are not man enough
To grasp your country's measure of a man.
If such as you, when Freedom's ways are rough,
Cannot walk in them, learn that women can!

Not yours, — because, in this the nation's need,
You stoop to bend her losses to your gain,
And do not feel the meanness of your deed; —
I touch no palm defiled with such a stain!

Whether man's thought can find too lofty steeps
  For woman's scaling, care not I to know;
But when he falters by her side, or creeps,
  She must not clog her soul with him to go.

Who weds me must at least with equal pace
  Sometimes move with me at my being's height:
To follow him to his superior place,
  His rarer atmosphere, were keen delight.

You lure me to the valley: men should call
  Up to the mountains, where the air is clear.
Win me and help me climbing, if at all!
  Beyond these peaks great harmonies I hear:—

The morning chant of Liberty and Law!
  The dawn pours in, to wash out Slavery's blot;
Fairer than aught the bright sun ever saw,
  Rises a Nation without stain or spot!

The men and women mated for that time
  Tread not the soothing mosses of the plain;
Their hands are joined in sacrifice sublime;
  Their feet firm set in upward paths of pain.

Sleep your thick sleep, and go your drowsy way!
  You cannot hear the voices in the air!
Ignoble souls will shrivel in that day;
  The brightness of its coming can you bear?

For me, I do not walk these hills alone:
  Heroes who poured their blood out for the truth,
Women whose hearts bled, martyrs all unknown,
  Here catch the sunrise of immortal youth

On their pale cheeks and consecrated brows:—
  It charms me not, your call to rest below.
I press their hands, my lips pronounce their vows:
  Take my life's silence for your answer: No!

RE-ENLISTED.

[May, 1864.]

O DID you see him in the street, dressed up in
army-blue,
When drums and trumpets into town their storm
of music threw, —
A louder tune than all the winds could muster in
the air,
The Rebel winds, that tried so hard our flag in
strips to tear?

You did n't mind him? O, you looked beyond him
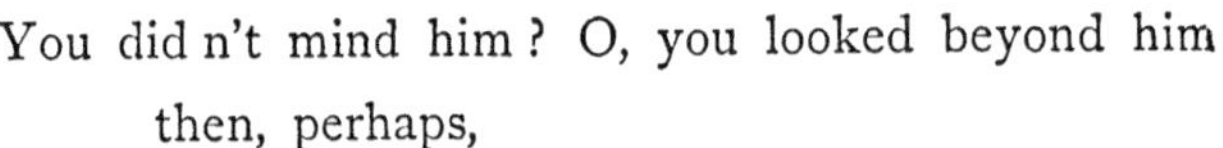
then, perhaps,
To see the mounted officers rigged out with trooper-
caps,
And shiny clothes, and sashes, and epaulets and
all; —
It was n't for such things as these he heard his
country call.

She asked for men; and up he spoke, my hand-
some, hearty Sam,
"I 'll die for the dear old Union, if she 'll take me
as I am."
And if a better man than he there 's mother that
can show,
From Maine to Minnesota, then let the nation
know.

You would not pick him from the rest by eagles
or by stars,
By straps upon his coat-sleeve, or gold or silver bars;
Nor a corporal's strip of worsted, but there 's some-
thing in his face,
And something in his even step, a-marching in his
place,

That could n't be improved by all the badges in
the land:
A patriot, and a good, strong man; are generals
much more grand?
We rest our pride on that big heart wrapped up
in army-blue,
The girl he loves, Mehitabel, and I, who love him
too.

He s never shirked a battle yet, though frightful
risks he 's run,
Since treason flooded Baltimore, the spring of Sixty-
One ;
Through blood and storm he 's held out firm, nor
fretted once, my Sam,
At swamps of Chickahominy, or fields of Antietam.

Though many a time, he 's told us, when he saw
them lying dead,
The boys that came from Newburyport, and Lynn,
and Marblehead,
Stretched out upon the trampled turf, and wept on
by the sky,
It seemed to him the Commonwealth had drained
her life-blood dry.

"But then," he said, "the more 's the need the
country has of me:
To live and fight the war all through, what glory
it will be!
The Rebel balls don't hit me ; and, mother, if they
should,
You 'll know I 've fallen in my place, where I have
always stood."

He 's taken out his furlough, and short enough it
seemed :
I often tell Mehitabel he 'll think he only dreamed
Of walking with her nights so bright you could n't
see a star,
And hearing the swift tide come in across the
harbor bar.

The Stars that shine above the Stripes, they light
him southward now ;
The tide of war has swept him back ; he 's made
a solemn vow
To build himself no home-nest till his country's
work is done ;
God bless the vow, and speed the work, my pa-
triot, my son !

And yet it is a pretty place where his new house
might be ; —
An orchard-road that leads your eye straight out
upon the sea.
The boy not work his father's farm ? it seems al-
most a shame ;
But any selfish plan for him he 'd never let me
name.

He 's re-enlisted for the war, for victory or for death, —
A soldier's grave, perhaps! — the thought has half-way stopped my breath,
And driven a cloud across the sun; — my boy, it will not be!
The war will soon be over; home again you 'll come to me!

He 's re-enlisted: and I smiled to see him going, too!
There 's nothing that becomes him half so well as army-blue.
Only a private in the ranks! but sure I am indeed,
If all the privates were like him, they 'd scarcely captains need.

And I and Massachusetts share the honor of his birth, —
The grand old State! to me the best in all the peopled earth!
I cannot hold a musket, but I have a son who can;
And I 'm proud for Freedom's sake to be the mother of a man!

CANTICLE DE PROFUNDIS.

GLORY to Thee, Father of all the Immortal,
Ever belongs:
We bring Thee from our watch by the grave's portal
Nothing but songs.
Though every wave of trouble has gone o'er us, —
Though in the fire
We have lost treasures time cannot restore us, —
Though all desire
That made life beautiful fades out in sorrow; —
Though the strange path
Winding so lonely through the bleak to-morrow,
No comfort hath; —
Though blackness gathers round us on all faces,
And we can see
By the red war-flash but Love's empty places; —
Glory to Thee!

For, underneath the crash and roar of battle,
The deafening roll

That calls men off to butchery like cattle,
Soul after soul, —
Under the horrid sound of chaos seething
In blind, hot strife,
We feel the moving of Thy Spirit, breathing
A better life
Into the air of our long-sickened nation;
A muffled hymn; —
The star-sung prelude of a new creation; —
Suffusions dim, —
The bursting upward of a stifled glory,
That shall arise
To light new pages in the world's great story
For happier eyes.

If upon lips too close to dead lips leaning,
Songs be not found,
Yet wilt Thou know our life's unuttered meaning:
In its deep ground,
As seeds in earth, sleep sorrow-drenched praises,
Waiting to bring
Incense to Thee along thought's barren mazes
When Thou send'st spring.

Glory to Thee! we say, with shuddering wonder,
While a hushed land
Hears the stern lesson syllabled in thunder,
That Truth is grand
As life must be; that neither man nor nation
May soil thy throne
With a soul's life-blood — horrible oblation! —
Nor quick be shown
That thou wilt not be mocked by prayer whose nurses
Were Hate and Wrong;
That trees so vile must drop back fruit in curses
Bitter and strong.

Glory to Thee, who wilt not let us smother
Ourselves in sin;
Sending Pain's messengers fast on each other
Us thence to win!
Praise for the scourging under which we languish,
So torn, so sore!
And save us strength, if yet uncleansed by anguish,
To welcome more.
Life were not life to us, could they be fables, —
Justice and Right:
Scathe crime with lightning, till we see the tables
Of Law burn bright!

Glory to Thee, whose glory and whose pleasure
Must be in good!
By Thee the mysteries we cannot measure
Are understood.
With the abysses of Thyself above us,—
Our sins below,—
That Thou dost look from Thy pure heaven and love us,
Enough to know.
Enough to lay our praises on Thy bosom;
Praises fresh-grown
Out of our depths, dark root and open blossom,
Up to thy throne.
When choking tears make our Hosannas falter,
The music free!
O keep clear voices singing at Thy altar,
Glory to Thee!

TOLLING.

[April 15, 1865.]

TOLLING, tolling, tolling!
All the bells of the land!
Lo! the patriot martyr
Taketh his journey grand;
Travels into the ages,
Bearing a hope how dear!
Into life's unknown vistas,
Liberty's great pioneer.

Tolling, tolling, tolling!
Do the budded violets know
The pain of the lingering clangor
Shaking their bloom out so?
They open into strange sorrow,
The rain of a nation's tears;
Into the saddest April
Twined with the New World's years.

Tolling, tolling, tolling!
  See, they come as a cloud,—
Hearts of a mighty people,
  Bearing his pall and shroud!
Lifting up, like a banner,
  Signals of loss and woe!
Wonder of breathless nations,
  Moveth the solemn show.

Tolling, tolling, tolling!
  Was it, O man beloved,—
Was it thy funeral only,
  Over the land that moved?—
Veiled by that hour of anguish,
  Borne with the Rebel rout,
Forth into utter darkness,
  Slavery's corse went out.

THE FLAG.

[JUNE 17, 1865.]

LET it idly droop, or sway
  To the wind's light will;
Furl its stars, or float in day;
  Flutter, or be still!
It has held its colors bright,
  Through the war-smoke dun;
Spotless emblem of the Right,
  Whence success was won.

Let it droop in graceful rest
  For a passing hour, —
Glory's banner, last and best;
  Freedom's freshest flower!
Each red stripe has blazoned forth
  Gospels writ in blood;
Every star has sung the birth
  Of some deathless good.

Let it droop, but not too long!
  On the eager wind

Bid it wave, to shame the wrong,
  To inspire mankind
With a larger human love;
  With a truth as true
As the heaven that broods above
  Its deep field of blue.

In the gathering hosts of hope,
  In the march of man,
Open for it place and scope,
  Bid it lead the van;
Till beneath the searching skies,
  Martyr-blood be found,
Purer than our sacrifice,
  Crying from the ground:—

Till a flag with some new light
  Out of Freedom's sky,
Kindles, through the gulfs of night,
  Glory yet more high.
Let its glow the darkness drown!
  Give our banner sway;
Till its joyful stars go down,
  In undreamed-of day!

MISCELLANEOUS.

K

HAND IN HAND WITH ANGELS.

HAND in hand with angels,
  Through the world we go;
Brighter eyes are on us
  Than we blind ones know;
Tenderer voices cheer us
  Than we deaf will own;
Never, walking heavenward,
  Can we walk alone.

Hand in hand with angels,
  In the busy street,
By the winter hearth-fires,—
  Everywhere,—we meet,
Though unfledged and songless,
  Birds of Paradise;
Heaven looks at us daily
  Out of human eyes.

Hand in hand with angels;
  Oft in menial guise;
By the same strait pathway
  Prince and beggar rise.
If we drop the fingers,
  Toil-imbrowned and worn,
Then one link with heaven
  From our life is torn.

Hand in hand with angels:
  Some are fallen, — alas!
Soiled wings trail pollution
  Over all they pass.
Lift them into sunshine!
  Bid them seek the sky!
Weaker is your soaring,
  When they cease to fly.

Hand in hand with angels;
  Some are out of sight,
Leading us, unknowing,
  Into paths of light.
Some dear hands are loosened
  From our earthly clasp,

Soul in soul to hold us
  With a firmer grasp.

Hand in hand with angels,—
  'T is a twisted chain,
Winding heavenward, earthward,
  Linking joy and pain.
There 's a mournful jarring,
  There 's a clank of doubt,
If a heart grows heavy,
  Or a hand 's left out.

Hand in hand with angels
  Walking every day;—
How the chain may lengthen,
  None of us can say.
But we know it reaches
  From earth's lowliest one,
To the shining seraph,
  Throned beyond the sun.

Hand in hand with angels!
  Blessed so to be!
Helped are all the helpers;
  Giving light, they see.

He who aids another
  Strengthens more than one;
Sinking earth he grapples
  To the Great White Throne.

EUREKA.

I RAN through a garden of roses at morning,
Uncaring the whither or why,
When, sudden as light, came a musical warning,
Thrilling over my heart like a sigh.
"Seek! seek!" one low word, and there followed no other:—
I gathered a white lily-bell;
A doveling I caught, newly left by its mother;
I stooped for a pebble, a shell.
But just as a joyous "Eureka!" replied,
My dove flew away, and my white lily died;
My pebble and shell lost the light of the wave,
And "I have not found," was the answer I gave.

Then outward I sally, a fearless crusader,
With "Seek" for a herald and guide.
On Error's dominions I march, an invader;
Green laurels the promise of Pride.

Impatient Goliath is striding to battle;
My foes are but pygmies to-day;
"Eureka!" I shout, while the war-thunders rattle, —
The victor rides forth from the fray.
"Eureka!" why falters my tongue at the word?
Chimæra yields not to a mortal's dull sword.
Lo, giants arise from the blood of the slain!
Alike were the search and the struggle in vain.

Now bring my good staff, for the pilgrim sees yonder
A Mecca, an altar of rest.
Beside that calm shrine I will seat me and ponder
And be in my solitude blest.
There Peace shall bend over me, Peace, the white angel
And Love, with her warm brooding wings.
Eureka! I hear it — a soothing evangel —
'T is gentle Reflection that sings.
Still cheated! Ixion still grasps at a cloud.
The white robe of Peace, — it is only a shroud!
My Mecca I leave; all in vain have I sought
The garden, the battle, the shrine; — they are naught.

Now pausing, a wanderer restless yet weary,
"Seek! seek!" how it sounds, like a moan!

Ah, where? for around all is barren and dreary;
  Beyond lies the dread, the unknown.
And upward — O, joy! what a glory is breaking!
  Why looked I not upward before?
My soul like a planet in sunlight is waking,
  To suffer eclipse nevermore.
Eureka! all dazzled with splendor I stand;
Light upward and inward, a Father at hand,
A crown overhead that erelong I shall win; —
Eureka! the Kingdom of God is within!

PSYCHE AT SCHOOL.

YOUNG Psyche came to school,
Down here in Being's lower vestibule,
Where many voices unto her did call
"Welcome! be studious! and in Mammon's hall
Shalt thou cup-bearer be to Mammon-King."
Thought Psyche, "No such thing!"

A volume Pleasure brought,
Of glowing pictures in earth-colors wrought.
Temptation's alphabet in ambush lay
Among the leaves; but Psyche turned away,
And said, "Those tints are mixed with poisonous paint;
It makes me sick and faint."

Then one approached, called Love,
Whose fingers o'er illumined print did move.
Psyche looked on and sighed: "The page is vext;
Your notes and your translations mar the text.

The angels write Love's idioms on the heart;
They are not learned by art."

Pride took an ancient book,
To teach the high-bred air, the scornful look.
Psyche returned her gaze with meek surprise,
And said, "Mine are not glass, but real eyes,
And will not stare like dead men's; since I see,
I cannot learn of thee."

"The child rebels," said Pride,
"Now be the lash by some rough teacher plied."
Then Poverty her rudest blows did give;
Said Psyche, "Pain assures me that I live.
"My robes are torn; but courage, faith, and love,
My triple mail, I prove."

Grief brought a scroll, writ o'er
With ink of nightshade and of hellebore.
Its damps were rainbows under Psyche's smile.
Despair with black tome open stood the while,
But said, "Her eyes would make the page too bright,"
And stole away from sight.

A guest undid the gate;
One who expects no welcome, soon or late.
Then Psyche took the parchment that he bore,
And whispered, gliding by him through the door,
"Kind Death, best friend! 't is my diploma given;
A graduate for heaven."

GODSENDS.

NOT the windfall makes us rich,
  But the slowly ripened fruit,
Full of sun-warmed nectar, which
  Drops, a patient need to suit.

Mean is every bauble brought,
  Favor of the mean to buy.
Offer us no gift unfraught
  With the largeness of the sky.

Offer but the breadth of love;
  Narrower boon is none at all.
Search for us the deeps above;
  Not the soil where earth-worms crawl.

Give the glory of a flower;
  Radiant leaf-bough; blooming thorn;
Light that seas and mountains shower;
  Rosy cheer of days new-born.

God sends what the true heart brings:
  Stranger or familiar hand,
Priest among His holy things,
  Only bears the gift He planned.

And the best of all He sends
  Is no measured dole, but love;
Is not cumbering goods, but friends;
  Winged souls with ours to move.

Soon we tire of pleasure's toy;
  Flashes o'er us, while we grope,
Glory of remoter joy;
  Beckoning of a larger hope:

Far as dreams, yet close at hand;
  Worlds unveiled in one soul's bound, —
Riches of the sun-vaults grand
  At your threshold may be found.

Learn the fools' gold to despise;
  Coinage of heaven's mint to know
In the home-illuming eyes;
  In the fireside's quiet glow;

In the roof-tree's timid bud;
  Hues that near horizons wear;
Planets your own sky that stud;
  Your own window's breath of air.

Naught but light from loftiest star;
  Naught than life more rare or new.
All the real Godsends are
  Common as the daily dew.

THIRTY-FIVE.

THE sun hangs calm at summer's poise;
The earth lies bathed in shimmering noon,
At rest from all her cheerful noise,
With heartstrings silently in tune.

The time, how beautiful and dear,
When early fruits begin to blush,
And the full leafage of the year
Sways o'er them with a sheltering hush!

The clouds that fleck the warm, blue deep
Like shoals of tinted fishes float;
From breathless groves the birds asleep
Send now and then a dreaming note.

A traveller through the noonday calm,
Not weary, yet in love with rest,
Glad of the air's refreshing balm,
Stays where yon threshold waits a guest.

Her half-way house of life is this:
  She sees the road wind up from far;
From the soft dells of childhood's bliss,
  Where twinkles home's remembered star

She feels that glimmer, out of sight,—
  A tender radiance of the past,
That drowned itself in deeper light;
  A joy that Joy forbade to last.

O morn of Spring! O green, green fields!
  Pressed by white feet of innocence!
The lilies that young verdure shields
  Yet send a pure, faint sweetness thence.

Those lilies yet perfume her heart;
  That morning lingers in her eye:
From God's first gifts she will not part,—
  Half the sweet light she travels by.

Yet think not she would wander back
  For childhood pure or merrier youth.
A mist is on the fading track,
  Here rounds the brightening orb of truth.

Nor painless can she look behind,
  On pitfalls that she did not shun;
Sure paths her heart refused to find;
  And guides that led her from the sun.

Then good seemed false, and evil true;
  Now out of evil blossoms good;
Life maps into a broader view,
  Its needed shadows understood.

Here at the half-way house of life,
  Upon these summer highlands raised,
Her thoughts are quieted from strife,
  Peace grows wherever she has gazed.

The spirit of the beauteous Now
  She deeply quaffs, for future strength,
And forward leans her shaded brow
  To scan the journey's waiting length.

Not down-hill all the afternoon;
  Though hides the path in many a vale,
It upward winds to sunset soon;
  To mountain summits far and pale.

Though lone those mountains seem, and cold,
  To such as know not of her Guide,
He gently leads to Love's warm fold;
  She sees them from their heaven-lit side.

And of the way that lies between,
  The mystery is the loveliest thing.
All yet a miracle has been,
  And life shall greater wonders bring.

The soul to God's heart moving on,
  Owns but the Infinite for home;
Whatever with the past has gone,
  The best is always yet to come.

'T will not be growing old, to feel
  The spirit, like a child, led on
By unseen presences, that steal
  For earth the light of heavenly dawn.

'T will not be terrible to bear
  Of inward pain the heaviest blow,
Since thus the rock is smitten, where
  Fountains of strength perennial flow.

To wait — to suffer — or to do;
  Each key unlocks its own deep bliss;
For every grief a comfort new; —
  A mine for gems the heart may miss.

Thus on she looks, with thoughts that sing
  Of happy months that follow June:
Life were not a completed thing,
  Without its summer afternoon;

Without its summery autumn hours; —
  That softened, spiritual time,
When o'er bright woods and frost-born flowers
  The seasons ring their perfect chime.

The time to bless and to be blest;
  For gathering and bestowing fruit;
When grapes are waiting to be pressed,
  And storms have fixed the tree's firm root.

Heaven's inmost sunshine earth has warmed;
  Heaven's peace floods each dark mystery;
And all the present glows, transformed,
  In the fair light of what shall be.

The traveller girds her to depart;
 She turns her toward the setting sun:
With morning's freshness in her heart,
 Her evening journey is begun.

SLEEP-SONG.

HUSH the homeless baby's crying,
Tender Sleep!
Every folded violet
May the outer storm forget.
Those wet lids with kisses drying,
Through them creep.

Soothe the soul that lies thought-weary,
Murmurous Sleep;
Like a hidden brooklet's song,
Rippling gorgeous woods among,
Tinkling down the mountains dreary,
White and steep.

Breathe thy balm upon the lonely,
Gentle Sleep;
As the twilight breezes bless
With sweet scents the wilderness:
Ah, let warm, white dove-wings only
Round them sweep!

O'er the aged pour thy blessing,
        Holy Sleep;
    Like a soft and ripening rain,
    Falling on the yellow grain:
For the glare of suns oppressing,
        Pitying weep!

On thy still seas met together,
        Charmed Sleep;
    Hear them swell a drowsy hymning,
    Swans to silvery music swimming,
Floating with unruffled feather
        O'er the deep.

SO LITTLE.

'TIS little we can look for now;
  The summer years are past;
The air is thick with coming snow,
  And dead leaves, falling fast.
A lonelier sound is in the wind,
For withered roses left behind.

There was an Indian summer, sweet
  With blossoms, faint and few,
When fruits lay ripened at our feet;
  But that has faded, too.
Its joy was but the after-glow
Of sunsets crimsoned long ago.

And yet we never plucked the flowers
  That budded in our dreams:
Even at the best, this world of ours
  Is other than it seems.
A generous world indeed it is, —
Most generous in its promises,

And with a golden promise still,
  It lures us travellers on
To death's white steep, the wintry hill
  Up which our friends have gone,
And vanished from our mortal sight,—
Thank God! into no starless night.

Faint music from beyond that steep;—
  A rose-breath, far and rare:—
So little can we guess!—but deep
  Heart's faith is rooted there.
So little,—and yet so much more
Than we have hoped or dreamed before!

THREE OLD SAWS.

IF the world seems cold to you,
  Kindle fires to warm it!
Let their comfort hide from view
  Winters that deform it.
Hearts as frozen as your own
  To that radiance gather.
You will soon forget to moan
  "Ah! the cheerless weather!"

If the world 's a wilderness,
  Go, build houses in it!
Will it help your loneliness
  On the winds to din it?
Raise a hut, however slight;
  Weeds and brambles smother;
And to roof and meal invite
  Some forlorner brother.

If the world 's a vale of tears,
  Smile, till rainbows span it!
Breathe the love that life endears,
  Clear of clouds to fan it.
Of your gladness lend a gleam
  Unto souls that shiver;
Show them how dark Sorrow's stream
  Blends with Hope's bright river.

A WORD WITH MY SOUL.

SOUL, what wisdom hast thou won,
Since thine earth-house was begun,
From loss of precious things,
And fair refurnishings?
Of all the guests that came and went,
Leaving their calm or discontent?
From crumblings of decay,—
New openings unto day?

Wouldst thou, soul, escape thy Past?
Life's foundation holds it fast.
The purity, the sin,
Alike are grounded in:
Therefrom doth lovely leafage spring;
Thence creepeth mould and tottering.
Whatso lies stifled there
Bring boldly to the air.

Soul, no Past can shelter thee:
Pleasant though its rooms may be,
    Opening unto earth,
    Filled with bloom and mirth,
To-day thou dost in vain return
To kindle fires that will not burn:
    As vainly shut its doors,
    Or veil its haunted floors.

Soul, thou hast arisen now
To the Present's sunnier glow:
    Thy windows are flung wide
    To light, on every side:
Beloved comrades gather here,
For work, and company, and cheer.
    Look in or out, and own
    How fair thy world has grown.

Sayest thou, Soul, "Here will I live;
Peace enjoy, and blessings give"?
    Tarriers of a day,
    Dear guests will not stay:
Wild winter comes: thy vines are bare:
Storm-beaten walls need large repair:

Night curtains thy glad room;
Shrouds thee in lonely gloom.

Build up, Soul, a lofty stair;
Build a room in healthier air.
Here there is no rest:
Better climbs to best.
Thy friends shall be the eternal stars;
They greet thee through thy casement bars:
Thy homesick feet they lead
Where thou no house wilt need.

Learn thou, Soul of mine, past doubt,
Thou canst all things do without:
All that through thy Past
Winds and clings so fast:
Sweet pictures hidden with a sigh,
As far too perfect to put by;
And all the wealth of thought
Into thy Present wrought.

From that height, Soul, thou shalt see,
In thy sky-tower, pluming thee

For unfettered flight
Through the fields of light,
The beauty of thine earthly nest,
As never, while it gave thee rest:
Yea, in thyself shalt find
Joy that seemed left behind.

THE WEEPING PROPHET.[4]

WOE, woe is me for my dear country's sin!
  Woe, that a prophet's torch was given to me
To hold up, hid God's shadowing light within,
  Before a people who refuse to see
How guilt draws down that light in burning levin;
How awful is the purity of heaven.

A boy among the hills of Anathoth
  I saw the visionary caldron seethe,
The almond-tree its ominous blossoms wreathe,
  In token that a righteous God was wroth
With Israel, and in judgment would condemn
The city of His love, Jerusalem.

To be his messenger of wrath I shrank:
  I cried, "O Lord, I am a child, so weak!
Who bears a curse, none give God-speed, or thank."
  Then did He touch my lips, His words I speak;
And, knowing that His eyes are on the truth,
I cannot answer evil ways with ruth.

Therefore I sit a mourner, and mine eyes
  Pour day and night their heavy sorrows down.
My people pass me by, for they despise
  His goodness, and with scoffs His warnings drown.
While o'er my head, in cloudy columns low,
The birds of prey that scent their ruin go.

Was ever any sorrow like to mine?
  It is no selfish trouble that I weep,
O daughter of my people, but I keep
  Vigil for thee, beneath the wrath divine,
The love that reddens into justice, when
God's perfect law is made the mock of men.

For, evermore, the tables of that law,
  Broken by man, are back upon him hurled.
O virgin daughter, thee defiled I saw,
  Wandering from Him, an outcast in the world,
Filthy without, and vile and crushed within;
A by-word through the ages for thy sin.

Alike in visions of the day and night,
  A spectral presence, not to be shut out,
A bleeding shadow, chased by shame and doubt,
  Hither and thither past me takes its flight

Into the unsheltering dark of east and west:—
A phantom, yet in faded splendors drest.

For thou wert beautiful, Jerusalem!
  Celestial colors wrapped thee at thy birth;
Kings pressed from far to kiss thy garment's hem,
  Chosen of God, a glory in the earth!
Falling from such a height to such a deep,—
To be the prophet of thy doom I weep!

NATURE AND THE BOOK.

I HEARD one say but now: "Shut up the Book;
  For Nature tells the story better still.
The fingered pages have a musty look;
  The wide green margins of the mountain rill,
The running notes of ripples on the beach,
  The open scroll of the blue firmament,
In loftier language the same lesson teach.
  Will not the broader truth thy mind content?
The cover of thy book may be a door
  To shut the elder gospel out of sight.
It tells thee only that which WAS before;
  God said, ere it was writ, 'Let there be light!'
And light is everywhere, — around, within;
  Earth luminous with heaven: what more wilt ask?
The Eternal Effluence is thy next of kin:
  Lay clogs aside, and in full freedom bask."

The Book lay open on the window-sill,
  And morning-glories leaned across the leaf

Whereon is written "Whosoever will";
  Also that story which hath lightened grief,
And dried within its source the mourner's tear;
  The story of a City built of light
Transmitted through all precious lustres clear,
  Within whose gem-walled streets shall be no night!

The morning-glories let the sunrise through,
  Shedding a various glow upon the Word:
With sumptuous lines of purple, red, and blue,
  Familiar promises were underscored.
I read and mused until my heart spoke out:
  "Nature saith 'Is,' but addeth not 'Shall be,'
Which God hath written here past any doubt;
  The words that human eyes ached long to see.

We might have guessed it. Some, the saintly-strong
  And clear of insight, know that unto life,
Which is of Him, His endless years belong,
  And are at rest from inward questioning strife.

"But few live on the mountain-peaks of thought,
  And fewer still keep holy instinct pure:
To sin, as unto weakness, hath He brought
  This lamp, to make the homeward pathway sure.

Shall we blow out our torch, because the sun
  Shone yesterday, and will to-morrow shine?
Too much of work remaineth to be done,
  And every gleam we toil by is divine.

"Wherefore should He permit these flowers to bloom,
  That rays from earth's great luminary break?
Because to us its dazzling blaze were gloom:
  Of ravelled rainbows beauty's web we make.
Jewel and blossom, shaded leaf and star
  Give no full revelation of the light.
Colors but letters of an alphabet are,
  Pointing us backward to the primitive white.
The common eye needs every tint and tone;
  The soul of man, much more, God's faintest word.
His glory through our mortal thought hath shone;
  When saint or prophet speaks, He still is heard:
And in the Revelation of the Book,—
  For surely He most brother-like hath come,—
As in a mirror on His face we look,
  So reassured, when Nature seemeth dumb.

"Yet will I listen to the ancient Voice,
  Forever new, that speaks in wind and wave;

It *is* the self-same tale ; let me rejoice
  In joy that His bewildered children have.
For they are glad in Him, the God Unknown :
  O that they knew the sacred emphasis
The Word on Nature's loveliness has thrown,
  And how the world by Christ's face lighted is,—
As if new sunshine brake into the air,—
  As if fresh odors burst from everything !
This Book is a wide window, opening fair
  Into the splendors of immortal Spring.
Nor shall it now be shut again on earth
  Until that City, that dear Bride, descends,
All souls resound the heavenly marriage-mirth,
  And all the blindness sin has brought us ends."

SABBATH DAYS.

THE dear old Sabbath days,
The quiet Sabbath days of long ago!
Across these shadeless ways
The upstart mornings boldly come and go.
None lingers on our gaze, —
No Sabbath now will shine upon us so.

Those gentle days are gone,
At our unworthy doors their dust off-shaken.
No more that noiseless dawn,
For which no other dawn could be mistaken, —
The reverent night withdrawn, —
Looks at us with calm eyes, till we awaken.

If any straggler walked
Through the hushed town, he met a spirit there,
That with his conscience talked
In low upbraidings, murmured through the air.
The very wild birds flocked
To the safe shelter of the house of prayer

The little ones, who went
By twos, in larger footprints, up the lane,
Paused as the shepherd bent
Crossed the worn threshold, leaning on his cane:
While the rich orchard-scent
Passed in and mingled with the psalm's clear strain.

The sun, slow moving round,
Looked from the bending heavens approval sweet.
There was no jarring sound;
The hours took off the sandals from their feet,
For earth seemed holy ground,—
A temple where the soul her God could meet.

But now the Sabbath sun
Shines quick and keen, as in the hurrying week;
And earthly noises stun
The spirit that would heaven in silence seek.
The praise for hire is done,
While their own thoughts the people think and speak.

'T is true that every hour
Is sacred to the earnest worshipper,

And every humble flower
Is Nature's text, to those who wait on her:
But those old days had power
The sluggish soul's Bethesda-pool to stir.

The Sabbath day! how well
The Pilgrims loved it, for the peace it brought!
We in the shadow dwell
Of its pavilion, for our shelter wrought.
Why break our holiest spell?
Why count the good old Sabbath days for naught?

A WHITE SUNDAY.

I ENTERED not the church this good Lord's Day,
Albeit my heart was with the worshippers,
Who stood beneath the arched and frescoed roof,
And sang to Him arisen. The same song
I heard innumerable happy birds
Trilling outside my window, in the boughs,
Among the blossoms; — and the blossoms sang, —
I dreamed it not, — "The Lord is risen indeed."
Surely there never fell so pure a light
From any crystalline cathedral-dome,
As that borne down with the soft summer rain
Through the pink apple-blooms, the lucid green
Of June's uncankered leaves, and branches gray,
Scutcheoned with lichens, tracery more antique
Than earls or bishops bear upon their shields.

A color not of earth, a tenderness
Of spotless snow and rose-bloom, clothed the tree,
That stood up underneath the heavens, one flower.

The multitude that John saw in white robes,
Singing the Heart Divine whose living drops
Had cleansed their stains, and warmed them into life,—
That multitude looked through my window-panes,
And with them I joined praises.
Friends devout,
Who listen to the sermon, swell the hymn,
Also the Lord accepts my offering.
To-day I worship in the apple-boughs,
With the great congregation of the flowers
That come up to their heights, as came the tribes
Of old unto Mount Zion, once a year;
A Passover of perfect, open praise.

The world we live in wholly is redeemed;
Not man alone, but all that man holds dear:
His orchards and his maize; forget-me-not
And heart's-ease in his garden; and the wild
Aerial blossoms of the untamed wood,
That make its savagery so home-like; all
Have felt Christ's sweet love watering their roots:
His sacrifice has won both earth and heaven.
Nature, in all its fulness, is the Lord's.
There are no Gentile oaks, no Pagan pines;

The grass beneath our feet is Christian grass;
The wayside weed is sacred unto Him.
Have we not groaned together, herbs and men,
Struggling through stifling earth-weights unto light,
Earnestly longing to be clothed upon
With our high possibility of bloom?
And He, He is the Light, He is the Sun
That draws us out of darkness, and transmutes
The noisome earth-damp into heaven's own breath,
And shapes our matted roots, we know not how,
Into fresh leaves and strong, fruit-bearing stems;
Yea, makes us stand, on some consummate day,
Abloom in white transfiguration-robes.

We are but human plants, with power to shut
In upon self our own impoverished lives,
Refusing light and growth. Unthankfully
We flaunt our blossoms in the face of heaven,
As if they overshone the eternal Sun
That is their inspiration; as if we
Sat in ourselves, and decked ourselves with flowers;—
An infinite littleness of vanity.

My apple-tree, thou preachest better things;
Whispering from all thy multitudinous buds,

"To bloom is boundless freedom. It is life
From self enfranchised, opening every vein
To let in glory from above, and give
What we receive, in fragrance, color, fruit;
Life, which is heaven's: ourselves dead matter, else."

Some good men say, "We need theology."
Others, "Not so, religion is enough."
What if both are mistaken, — and both right?
GOD is our need, a Presence and a Life.
Theology enthrones him in the mind,
Yet sometimes leaves the heart as hard as stone,
The hands as lifeless. And Religion, too,
Is often only an ambiguous word
For transient fervor, or for duty cold,
Or vain, self-helpful works of charity.
Without Him thought is soulless; rapture blind;
Duty a lifelong bondage; love, thin air.
Through Him alone is man a living soul:
Through Him alone is earth the bride of heaven.

Here in Thy great world-garden, Lord, we stand:
And Thou, whose trees we are, who art our sun,
Hast once descended to our roots of being,

And bloomed and breathed in our humanity,
That we might be as Thou, and know no death.
The life we live is Thine, not ours. We bloom
To gladden earth with sacrifice like Thine,
So clad in Thy white robes of righteousness.
Keep us! for here the blossoms blight so fast!
The fruit is flawed in turning from Thy beams
To the biting east, to folly and to sin.
And let all trees, the wildings of the wood,
And grafts of rarest culture, waft Thee praise.

My apple-tree, thy dome of rose and pearl
Will vanish on the morrow, like a dream.
Yet every spring, the springs when I am dead,
A tabernacle thou wilt build for men;
And they will look up through thee into heaven,
And hear the hum of bees among thy boughs,
A faint sky-music. I shall worship then,
With friends beloved, under other shade.
Are only palms in Eden? I shall miss
The tree whereby Eve fell,—if that thou wert,—
Not seeing it beside the River of Life.
Thou art too beautiful to be dropped out
Of human vision, even beatified.

There is no glory of the trees like thine,
Though there be many set in Paradise;
There must thou blossom also.
                                        Dreams are lost
In guessing at the glory of thy boughs
In that immortal spring-time.
                                        Ah! dear friends,
Sweet memories of the earth, and sad no more,
Will float around us in the air of heaven,
A fragrance and a melody, when we,
Young, glad, and all as if at home again,
Sit under our transplanted apple-trees.

SONNETS.

I.

DROUGHT.

THERE is a trouble may befall the soul,
 Beside which grief will seem a happiness.
 The stream whose murmur evermore to bless
Your desert with bewildering music stole —
That o'er your waste of being did unroll
 A weft of green, for beauty and for shade,
 And in the wilderness a garden made —
Withdraws, drop after drop, its priceless dole;
 And the sweet grasses that the wind sang through,
And all the star-eyed blossoms, droop and die,
Till your bare life lies open to the sky, —
 The wide, calm weariness of rainless blue, —
Without a voice to babble its distress;
A barren, uncomplaining silentness.

II.

SPRINGS IN THE DESERT.

AND there is joy no music can express,
When in the empty channels of the heart
New springs of love from unknown sources start;
When all the desert-land of selfishness
That, parched and shrivelling in its own distress,
Sent not a drop to cheer the neighboring waste,
Breaks into song, and with o'erflowing haste
Pours rill to rill, a suffering soil to bless.
O silent, burning hearts! of lonely things
Your lot is far the mournfullest, the worst.
But when your sands with cooling waters burst,
Each thought in welcome of that wonder sings,
Spring up, O well! from God the fountain flows
That makes the desert blossom as the rose.

THE SECRET.

WHAT selfishness asked for
Was vain:
What came for that asking
Brought pain.

Heaven's manna in keeping
Was spoiled:
All beauty self-seeking
Hath soiled.

Complacency blazoned
Dull dross.
No gain came of hoarding,
But loss.

Gain! none save the giver
Receives.
Yet who that old gospel
Believes?

Nor pauper nor beggar
　　Then be ;
Nor niggard of bounty
　　Most free.

But one way is Godlike, —
　　To give.
Then pour out thy heart's blood,
　　And live !

"HIMSELF HE CANNOT SAVE."

O SCOFFER! He who from the cross
Looked down thy dark abysm of loss,
And knew His pain alone could win
Such souls as thine from gulfs of sin, —
His death-groan mournful echo gave:
"Myself I cannot save."

Words breathed in scorn, yet understood
By Him to bear a sense of good:
The secret of the glorious strife
Between the powers of death and life,
Love's deepest truth, — self-sacrifice, —
Hid in that mockery lies.

And he must understand it so
Who would relieve a brother's woe:
He cannot shun his own distress;
He hastes, with Christ-like earnestness,
Although the way be through his grave:
Himself he cannot save.

Some happy souls may pass along
The heavenward road with smile and song,
Through guileless infancy and youth
Linked in with followers of the truth;
And their unconsciousness of ill
But makes them lovelier still.

Their peaceful path is not for all:
Each must obey his separate call;
And he is of himself abhorred
Who flies the summons of the Lord:
Sailing from danger unto ease,
He sinks in unknown seas.

None longs so for yon vales of peace
As he whom war gives no release.
But exiles' chains his brethren wear;
He knows no rest they may not share;
For them all hardships he must brave:
Himself he cannot save.

Aye, through all pain and loneliness,
Where men are perilled, he must press
To rescue, crying, "Woe is me,

Resisting not the wrong I see!
If none uphold me, I must go
Singly against the foe!"

And not the warrior-heart alone
The scoffer's word for truth has known.
The mourner, weeping out the night
For aliens from the one true Light;
The watcher by the bed of pain,
Who knows her watch in vain;

He who has felt his heaviest cross
Far lighter than another's loss;
He who can ask and bear the blow
That shelters any soul from woe,
Sees why that Death on Calvary
Life's beacon-light must be.

Ring, mournful echo, through the world!
Float, banner of the Cross, unfurled
To show the servant who would prove
His Master's joy of suffering love,
That, while thy folds above him wave,
Himself he cannot save!

"AS STRANGERS AND PILGRIMS."

AS strangers, — glad for this good inn,
Where nobler wayfarers have been;
Yet asking but a little rest:
Earth may not keep her spirit-guest.

As those whom no entangling bond
Must draw from life and love beyond:
Strangers to all that lures astray
From one plain path, the homeward way.

How must the pilgrim's load be borne?
With staggering limbs, and look forlorn?
His Guide chose all that load within·
There's need of everything, but sin.

So, trusting Him whose love he knows,
Singing along the road he goes;
And nightly of his burden makes
A pillow till the morning breaks.

How thinks the pilgrim of his way?
As wanderers homesick and astray?—
The starlight and the dew he sees;
He feels the blessing of the breeze;

The valley-shades, how cool and still!
What splendor from the beetling hill!
He longs to go,—he loves to stay;—
For God is both his Home and Way.

Strangers to sin! beloved of God!
Ye track with heaven-light earth's mean sod;
For, pilgrims dear, HE walks with you,
A Guide,—but once a Pilgrim too.

MONICA AND AUGUSTINE.[5]

IN the martyr Cyprian's chapel there was moaning through the night;
Monica's low prayer stole upward till it met the early light.
Till the dawn came, walking softly o'er the troubled sea without,
Monica for her Augustine wept the dreary watches out.

"Lord of all the holy martyrs! Giver of the crown of flame,
Set on hoary-headed Cyprian, who to Thee child-hearted came;
Hear me for my child of promise! Thou his erring way canst see;
Long from Thee a restless wanderer, must he go away from me?

"'T is for Thee, O God, a motner this her wondrous child would keep;

Through the ripening of his manhood Thou hast
seen me watch and weep.
Tangled in the mesh of Mani, groping through the
maze of sense,
Other, deadlier snares await him, if from me he
wander hence.

"Thine he shall be, Lord; Thy promise brightens
up my night of fears:
Faith beholds him at Thy altar, yet baptized with
only tears;
For the angel of my vision, came he not from Thy
right hand,
Whispering unto me, his mother, 'Where thou
standest, he shall stand'?

"Saviour, Lord, whose name is Faithful, I am Thine,
I rest on Thee;
And beside me in Thy kingdom I this wanderer
shall see.
Check the tide! hold still the breezes! for his soul's
beloved sake,
Do not let him leave me! Keep him—keep him—
lest my heart should break!"

* * * * *

Man must ask, and God will answer, yet we may not understand,
Knowing but our own poor language, all the writing of His hand.
In our meagre speech we ask him, and He answers in His own;
Vast beyond our thought the blessing that we blindly judge is none.

When the sun rose from the water, Monica was on the shore;
Out of sight had dropped the vessel that afar Augustine bore.
Home she turned, her sad heart singing underneath its load of care,
"Still I know Thy name is faithful, O Thou God that hearest prayer!"

* * * * *

By the garden-beds of Ostia now together stand the twain,
Monica and her Augustine, gazing far across the main,

Toward the home-land of Numidia, hiding in the
distance dim,
Where God parted them in sorrow, both to bring
the nearer Him.

And the mother's prayer is answered, for their souls
are side by side,
Where His peace flows in upon them with a full
eternal tide.
And Augustine's thought is blending with the mur
mur of the sea;
"Bless Thee, Lord, that we are restless, till we find
our rest in Thee!"

And their talk, the son and mother, leaning out
above the flowers,
Is like lapse of angel-music, linking heaven's enrap-
tured hours.
Hushed is all the song of Nature; hushed is care,
and passion's din,
In that hush they hear a welcome from the High-
est:—"Enter in!"

"What new mercy has befallen? every earthly wish
is gone,"
Monica half speaks, half muses; "why should earthly
life move on?
Ah, my son, what peace and gladness surging from
this silence roll!
'T is the Eternal Deep that answers to the deep
within my soul!

'Not a sigh of homesick longing moves the still-
ness of my heart;
In the light of this great glory, unto God would I
depart.
Though more dear thou art than ever, standing at
heaven's gate with me,
For the sweetness of His presence I could say fare-
well to thee."

* * * * *

There 's a silent room in Ostia; tearless mourners
by a bed:
Since the angels roused that sleeper, who shall weep,
or call her dead?

Not beside the dust beloved shall her exiled ashes lie;
She awaits the Resurrection underneath a Roman sky.

Now Augustine in his bosom keeps the image of a saint,
Whose warm tears of consecration drop on thoughts of sinful taint.
In the home that knew him erring, a bewildered Manichee,
Minister at Truth's high altar, him that mother-saint shall see.

In the dreams of midnight, haunted by the ghosts of buried sins;.
In the days of calm, the spirit, struggling through temptation, wins;
Monica looks down upon him, joy to bless, and gloom beguile;
And the world can see Augustine clearer for that saintly smile.

Still the billows from Numidia seek the lovely Roman shore,

Though Augustine to his mother sailed long since
the death-wave o'er,
Still his word sweeps down the ages like the surging of the sea:
"Bless Thee, Lord, that we are restless, till we find
our rest in Thee!"

DEVOTIONAL.

A THANKSGIVING.

FOR the wealth of pathless forests,
  Whereon no axe may fall;
For the winds that haunt the branches;
  The young bird's timid call;
For the red leaves dropped like rubies
  Upon the dark green sod;
For the waving of the forests,
  I thank thee, O my God!

For the sound of waters gushing
  In bubbling beads of light;
For the fleets of snow-white lilies
  Firm-anchored out of sight;
For the reeds among the eddies;
  The crystal on the clod;
For the flowing of the rivers,
  I thank Thee, O my God!

For the rosebud's break of beauty
  Along the toiler's way;
For the violet's eye that opens
  To bless the new-born day;
For the bare twigs that in summer
  Bloom like the prophet's rod;
For the blossoming of flowers,
    I thank Thee, O my God!

For the lifting up of mountains,
  In brightness and in dread;
For the peaks where snow and sunshine
  Alone have dared to tread;
For the dark of silent gorges,
  Whence mighty cedars nod;
For the majesty of mountains,
  I thank Thee, O my God!

For the splendor of the sunsets,
  Vast mirrored on the sea;
For the gold-fringed clouds, that curtain
  Heaven's inner mystery;
For the molten bars of twilight,
  Where thought leans, glad, yet awed;

For the glory of the sunsets,
  I thank Thee, O my God!

For the earth, and all its beauty;
  The sky and all its light;
For the dim and soothing shadows,
  That rest the dazzled sight;
For unfading fields and prairies,
  Where sense in vain has trod;
For the world's exhaustless beauty,
  I thank Thee, O my God!

For an eye of inward seeing;
  A soul to know and love;
For these common aspirations,
  That our high heirship prove;
For the hearts that bless each other
  Beneath Thy smile, Thy rod;
For the amaranth saved from Eden,
  I thank Thee, O my God!

For the hidden scroll, o'erwritten
  With one dear Name adored;

For the Heavenly in the human;
  The Spirit in the Word;
For the tokens of Thy presence
  Within, above, abroad;
For Thine own great gift of Being,
  I thank Thee, O my God!

OUR PRAYERS.

ART Thou not weary of our selfish prayers?
  Forever crying, "Help me, save me, Lord!"
We stay fenced in by petty fears and cares,
  Nor hear the song outside, nor join its vast accord.

And yet the truest praying is a psalm:
  The lips that open in pure air to sing
Make entrance to the heart for health and balm;
  And so life's urn is filled at heaven's all-brimming
    spring.

Is not the need of other souls our need?
  After desire the helpful act must go,
As the strong wind bears on the winged seed
  To some bare spot of earth, and leaves it there
    to grow.

Still are we saying, "Teach us how to pray"?
  O teach us how to love! and then our prayer

Through other lives will find its upward way,
As plants together seek and find sweet life and air.

Thy large bestowing makes us ask for more.
Prayer widens with the world wherethrough love flows.
Needy, though blest, we throng before Thy door:
Let in Thy sunshine, Lord, on all that lives and grows!

AT THE BEAUTIFUL GATE.

LORD, open the door, for I falter,
I faint in this stifled air;
In dust and straitness I lose my breath;
This life of self is a living death:
Let me into Thy pastures broad and fair,
To the sun and the wind from Thy mountains free;
Lord, open the door to me!

There is holier life, and truer,
Than ever my heart has found:
There is nobler work than is wrought within
These walls so charred by the fires of sin,
Where I toil like a captive blind and bound:
An open door to a freer task
In Thy nearer smile, I ask.

Yet the world is Thy field, Thy garden;
On earth art Thou still at home.

When Thou bendest hither Thy hallowing eye,
My narrow work-room seems vast and high,
Its dingy ceiling a rainbow dome:—
Stand ever thus at my wide-swung door,
And toil will be toil no more.

Through the rosy portals of morning,
Now the tides of sunshine flow.
O'er the blossoming earth and the glistening sea,
The praise Thou inspirest rolls back to Thee:
Its tones through the infinite arches go;
Yet, crippled and dumb, behold me wait,
Dear Lord, at the Beautiful Gate.

I wait for Thy hand of healing,—
For vigor and hope in Thee.
Open wide the door,—let me feel the sun,—
Let me touch Thy robe:—I shall rise and run
Through Thy happy universe, safe and free,
Where in and out Thy beloved go,
Nor want nor wandering know.

Thyself art the Door, Most Holy!
By Thee let me enter in!

I press toward Thee with my failing strength:
Unfold Thy love in its breadth and length!
True life from thine let my spirit win!
To the Saints' fair City, the Father's Throne,
Thou, Lord, art the way alone.

From the deeps of unseen glory
Now I feel the flooding light.
O rare sweet winds from Thy hills that blow!
O River so calm in its crystal flow!
O Love unfathomed, — the depth, the height!
What joy wilt Thou not unto me impart,
When Thou shalt enlarge my heart!

To be made with Thee one spirit,
Is the boon that I lingering ask.
To have no bar 'twixt my soul and Thine;
My thoughts to echo Thy will divine;
Myself Thy servant, for any task.
Life! life! I may enter, through Thee, the Door, —
Saved, sheltered forevermore!

MY ANGEL-DRESS.

HEAVENLY Father, I would wear
 Angel-garments, white and fair:
Angel-vesture undefiled
Wilt Thou give unto thy child?

Not a robe of many hues,
Such as earthly fathers choose;—
Discord weaves the gaudy vest:
Not in such let me be drest.

Take the raiment soiled away
That I wear with shame to-day:
Give my angel-robe to me,
White with heavenly purity.

Take away my cloak of pride,
And the worthless rags 't would hide:
Clothe me in my angel-dress,
Beautiful with holiness.

Perfume every fold with love,
Hinting heaven where'er I move;
As an Indian vessel's sails
Whisper of her costly bales.

Let me wear my white robes here,
Even on earth, my Father dear,
Holding fast Thy hand, and so
Through the world unspotted go.

Let me now my white robes wear:
Then I need no more prepare,
All apparelled for my home
Whensoe'er Thou callest, "Come!"

Thus apparelled, I shall be
As a signal set for Thee,
That the wretched and the weak
May the same fair garments seek.

"Buy of Me," I hear Thee say:
I have naught wherewith to pay,
But I give myself to Thee;
Clothed, adopted I shall be.

"FOLLOW THOU ME."

O WHERE shall we follow Thee, Saviour beloved?
To Kedron, where oft thou hast thoughtfully roved?
—Each rill of enjoyment that winds through our care
Is Kedron, if Thou wilt but walk with us there.

O where shall we follow Thee, Jesus, our Friend?
To Bethany, whither thy feet loved to tend?
—Our fireside is Bethany, peaceful and blest;
And ne'er will we wander, with Thee for a guest.

O where shall we follow Thee, Master adored?
To the Beautiful City that knew not her Lord?
—Alas for our streets, full of evil and pain!
Toil with us for cities wept over in vain!

O where shall we follow Thee, Leader Divine?
To Tabor, where thou in white glory didst shine?
—Thy face in the sin-sick and weary we see,
When Love is the Tabor we stand on with Thee.

O where shall we follow Thee, tenderest Guide?
To the sweet, mournful garden down Olivet's side?
— Ah, here is Gethsemane,—here, where we mourn:
Here strengthen us, Thou who our sorrow hast
borne!

O where shall we follow Thee, dear Lamb of God?
Up Golgotha's death-steep, for us meekly trod?
—The thorns pierce our temples; the cross bears
us down;
Like Thine, make our Calvary garland our crown!

O where shall we follow Thee, conquering Lord?
To Paradise, unto us outcasts restored?
'T is Paradise, Lord, in thy presence to be;
And, living or dying, we 're ever with Thee!

THY WILL BE DONE.

ONLY silently resigned
To the counsels of Thy mind;
Willing, yet rejoicing not,
That Thy purpose shall be wrought;

Is this truly to submit?
Folding placid hands, to sit,
While innumerable feet
Thy triumphant coming meet?

Shall we say, "Thy will be done!"
And on our own errands run?
Vain and evil the design
We pursue, apart from Thine.

Teach us how to live this prayer;
Reverently Thy plans to share.
More than echoes of Thy voice, —
Make us partners in Thy choice.

Lift us up to catch from Thee
World-encircling sympathy.
Ardor, strength, and courage give;
As Thou livest, let us live!

Let our deeds be syllables
Of the prayer our spirit swells.
In us Thy desire fulfil;
By us work Thy gracious will!

THE STILL HOUR.

THE quiet of a shadow-haunted pool
Where light breaks through in glorious tenderness,
Where the tranced pilgrim in the shelter cool
Forgets the way's distress;

Such is this hour, this silent hour with Thee!
The trouble of the restless heart is still,
And every swaying wish breathes reverently
The whisper of Thy will.

Father, our thoughts are rushing wildly on,
Tumultuous, clouded with their own vain strife;
Darkened by cares from our own planting grown;—
We call the tumult life.

And something of Thy presence still is given:
The keen light flashing from the seething foam,

Through tangled boughs the sudden glimpse of
heaven,
From Thee, Thee only, come.

And beautiful it is to catch Thy smile
Amid the rush, the hurrying flow of mind;
To feel Thy glance upon us all the while,
Most holy and most kind!

But oh! this hour of heavenly quietness,
When, as a lake that opens to the sky,
The soul serene in its great blessedness
Looks up to meet Thine eye!

Fountain of Life, in Thee alone is Light!
Shine through our being, cleansing us of sin,
Till we grow lucid with Thy presence bright,
The peace of God within.

Yet not alone as Light pervading come;—
O Thou Divine One, meet us as a Friend!
Only with Thee is every heart at home:
Stay with us to the end!

By the stream's windings let us with Thee talk
  Of this strange earth-life Thou so well hast known
In Thy fresh footprints let us heavenward walk, —
    No more to grope alone!

If in our thoughts, by Thee made calm and clear,
  The brightening image of Thy face we see,
What hour of all our lives can be so dear
    As this still hour with Thee!

THE COMING LIFE.

HEAVEN'S NEED.

YE who, passing, bore away
Best of sunshine from our day,—
That rare glory which revives
On the sky of clouded lives,
When, through mists at evening rent,
Rays from inmost heaven are sent,—
What of earth to you remains,
Mid imperishable gains?

Mother-love, unchilled by change,
Absence wide, and coldness strange,—
Mother-love, that here must yearn
Vainly for its full return
From the shallow heart of youth,—
Art requited now, in truth?
Or does thy dumb longing go
Through heaven's happy overflow?

Sister-love, so calm, so wise!
Starlight, risen on darkened skies;
Heart that made its rifled nest
Shelter for the homeless guest,—
Of thy tenderness bereft,
Little warmth in life is left.
Has that new world's flood of bliss
Swept apart the ties of this?

None may name a drearier thought;—
Hearts we lean on need us not.
If they ask for us no more,
Gathering in heaven's affluent store,
Life is lonelier than we knew;
Sharper anguish thrills death through.
In this rubbish-heap of earth.
Hides no pearl heaven's saving worth?

God is good. His face they see,
And are glad eternally.
Yet they hear love's wordless prayer,—
Sigh that stirs the peaceful air,

And our yearning secret tells
To the bending asphodels.
Lacks one drop their cup to fill;
Still they want us, wait us still.

THE CHAMBER CALLED PEACE.[6]

ON a hill-top, divested of trouble, I rested,
One blue, starry night,
In a fair eastern chamber, where vines strove to clamber
And play in the light.
There star-beams, uncertain, crept down through a curtain
Of thin, airy fleece;
There, veiling her brightness in silvery whiteness,
The moonlight, caressing, stole in with a blessing,
To the chamber called Peace.

The mountains surrounding, with radiance abounding,
In the broad blaze of day,
Encircled my spirit, to strengthen and cheer it,
When the night-purple lay
Like a mantle upon them, and silence had won them,
Bold prophets, to cease

From their unfinished story of Infinite Glory:
But its echo, low-breathing, like incense came
wreathing
The chamber called Peace.

Though dripping November had quenched the last
ember
Of autumn's red fire,
A presence enchanted the forest yet haunted;
It could not expire:
It lit the leaves, flying from winds feebly sighing
For summer's decease;
Touched the birches white-fingered, that silently
lingered,
Where pine-choirs were sending an anthem un-
ending
Through the chamber called Peace.

In a still flood of amber, Dawn entered the chamber,
The sleeper to rouse.
A rose-cloud passed slowly, — a messenger holy,
At pause for the vows
Of pilgrims awaking; — then lifting and breaking
From a rich, robing fleece,

Like an Eye fondly glowing, a Heart overflowing,
The sun, proud and tender, lit up with full splendor
The chamber called Peace.

In that white, wayside dwelling, one pilgrim was swelling
Her heavenward lay.
The strength of the mountains, the joy of their fountains,
Had gladdened her stay:
The pine-trees' deep sighing, the wind's low replying,
For her soon would cease;
But a holier singing the angels were bringing
To her dawn-lighted chamber, all whiteness and amber,
Her chamber called Peace.

O, joy was it, staying where angels were playing
The sweet airs of heaven
To one blest immortal, whose rest at the portal
Half open, was given.
While we, scarcely grieving, awaited her leaving,
Her hour of release,

Hills and heavens around us, like walls seemed
to bound us,
Of a Home all unblighted, a Mansion love-lighted,
A chamber called Peace.

For, on earth or in heaven, to true hearts is given
One quiet abode;
One mighty Arm guards them, one blessing rewards
them, —
The Presence of God!
The stars in declining fail not of their shining,
Through daylight's increase:
They who pass on before us leave dawn break-
ing o'er us,
Lighting up, through death's grating, our cham-
ber of waiting,
Our chamber called Peace.

A YEAR IN HEAVEN.

ONE year among the angels, beloved, thou hast been;
One year has heaven's white portal shut back the sound of sin:
And yet no voice, no whisper, comes floating down from thee,
To tell us what glad wonder a year of heaven may be.

Our hearts before it listen, — the beautiful closed gate:
The silence yearns around us; we listen and we wait.
It is thy heavenly birthday, on earth thy lilies bloom;
In thine immortal garland canst find for these no room?

Thou lovedst all things lovely when walking with
us here;
Now, from the heights of heaven, seems earth no
longer dear?
We cannot paint thee moving in white-robed state
afar,
Nor dream our flower of comfort a cool and dis-
tant star.

Heaven is but life made richer: therein can be no
loss:
To meet our love and longing thou hast no gulf
to cross;
No adamant between us uprears its rocky screen;
A veil before us only; — thou in the light serene.

That veil 'twixt earth and heaven a breath might
waft aside;
We breathe one air, beloved, we follow one dear
Guide:
Passed in to open vision, out of our mists and rain,
Thou seest how sorrow blossoms; how peace is won
from pain.

And half we feel thee leaning from thy deep calm of bliss,
To say of earth, "Beloved, how beautiful it is!
The lilies in this splendor, — the green leaves in this dew; —
O, earth is also heaven, with God's light clothed anew!"

So, when the sky seems bluer, and when the blossoms wear
Some tender, mystic shading we never knew was there,
We'll say "We see things earthly by light of sainted eyes;
She bends where we are gazing, to-day, from Paradise."

Because we know thee near us, and nearer still to Him
Who fills thy cup of being with glory to the brim,
We will not stain with grieving our fair, though fainter light,
But cling to thee in spirit as if thou wert in sight.

And as in waves of beauty the swift years come
and go,
Upon celestial currents our deeper life shall flow,
Hearing, from that sweet country where blighting
never came,
Love chime the hours immortal, in earth and heaven
the same.

Q

BY THE FIRESIDE.

WHAT is it fades and flickers in the fire,
Mutters and sighs, and yields reluctant breath,
As if in the red embers some desire,
Some word prophetic, burned, defying death?

Lords of the forest, stalwart oak and pine,
Lie down for us in flames of martyrdom:
A human, household warmth, their death-fires shine;
Yet fragrant with high memories they come;

Bringing the mountain-winds that in their boughs
Sang of the torrent, and the plashy edge
Of storm-swept lakes; and echoes that arouse
The eagles from some splintered eyrie-ledge;

And breath of violets sweet about their roots;
And earthy odors of the moss and fern;
And hum of rivulets; smell of ripening fruits;
And green leaves that to gold and crimson turn.

What clear Septembers fade out in a spark!
What rare Octobers drop with every coal!
Within these costly ashes, dumb and dark,
Are hid spring's budding hope, and summer's soul.

Pictures far lovelier smoulder in the fire,
Visions of friends who walked among these trees,
Whose presence, like the free air, could inspire
A winged life and boundless sympathies.

Eyes with a glow like that in the brown beech,
When sunset through its autumn beauty shines;
Or the blue gentian's look of silent speech,
To heaven appealing as earth's light declines;

Voices and steps forever fled away
From the familiar glens, the haunted hills, —
Most pitiful and strange it is to stay
Without you in a world your lost love fills.

Do you forget us, — under Eden-trees,
Or in full sunshine on the hills of God, —
Who miss you from the shadow and the breeze,
And tints and perfumes of the woodland sod?

Dear for your sake the fireside where we sit
  Watching these sad, bright pictures come and go;
That waning years are with your memory lit,
  Is now the lonely comfort that we know.

Is it all memory? Lo, these forest-boughs
  Burst on the hearth into fresh leaf and bloom;
Waft a vague, far-off sweetness through the house,
  And give close walls the hillside's breathing-room.

A second life, more spiritual than the first,
  They find, a life won only out of death.—
O sainted souls, within you still is nursed
  For us a flame not fed by mortal breath.

Unseen, you bring to this, erewhile your home,
  Fresh air from the new country close above;
Through no oblivious heaven your footsteps roam;
  Alive in God, you bless us with His love.

NEAR SHORE.

THE seas of thought are deep and wide;
  Let those who will, O friend of mine,
Sail forth without a chart or guide,
  Or plummet-line;

A blank of waters all around, —
  A blank of azure overhead, —
An infinite of nothing found,
  Whence faith has fled.

The Name that we with reverence speak,
  Echoes across those wastes of thought:
But they who go far off to seek,
  They hear it not.

The shores give back its sweetest sound
  From rivulet cool, and shadowing rock,
And voices that calm hearths surround
  With friendly talk.

Earth is our little island home,
  And heaven the neighboring continent,
Whence winds to every inlet come
  With balmiest scent

And tenderest whispers thence we hear
  From those who lately sailed across.
They love us still; since heaven is near,
  Death is not loss.

From mountain slopes of breeze and balm,
  What melodies arrest the oar!
What memories ripple through the calm!
  We 'll keep near shore.

By sweet home instincts wafted on,
  By all the hopes that life has nursed,
We hasten where the loved have gone,
  Who landed first.

If God be God, then heaven is real:
  We need not lose ourselves and Him
In some vast sea of the ideal,
  Dreamy and dim.

He cheats not any soul. He gave
  Each being unity like His;
Love, that links beings, He must save;
        Of Him it is.

Dear friend, we will not drift too far
  Mid billows, fogs, and blinding foam,
To see Christ's beacon-light, — the star
        That guides us home.

Moving toward heaven, we 'll meet half-way
  Some pilot from that unseen strand;
Then, anchoring safe in perfect day,
        Tread the firm land.

Then onward and forever on
  Toward summits piled on summits bright.
The lost are found, and we have won
        The Land of Light!

God is that country's glory: He
  Alike the confidence is found
Of those who try the uncertain sea
        Or solid ground.

Yet we, for love of those who bend
  From yon clear heights, passed on before
To wait our coming, — we, dear friend,
        Will keep near shore.

ACROSS THE RIVER.

WHEN for me the silent oar
  Parts the Silent River,
And I stand upon the shore
  Of the strange Forever,
Shall I miss the loved and known?
Shall I vainly seek mine own?

Mid the crowd that come to meet
  Spirits sin-forgiven, —
Listening to their echoing feet
  Down the streets of heaven, —
Shall I know a footstep near
That I listen, wait for here?

Then will one approach the brink
  With a hand extended,
One whose thoughts I loved to think
  Ere the veil was rended,
Saying "Welcome! we have died,
And again are side by side."

Saying, "I will go with thee,
  That thou be not lonely,
To yon hills of mystery:
  I have waited only
Until now, to climb with thee
Yonder hills of mystery."

Can the bonds that make us here
  Know ourselves immortal,
Drop away, like foliage sear,
  At life's inner portal?
What is holiest below
Must forever live and grow.

I shall love the angels well,
  After I have found them
In the mansions where they dwell,
  With the glory round them.
But at first, without surprise,
Let me look in human eyes.

Step by step our feet must go
  Up the holy mountain;
Drop by drop, within us flow,
  Life's unfailing fountain.

Angels sing with crowns that burn;
We shall have a song to learn.

He who on our earthly path
  Bids us help each other —
Who his Well-beloved hath
  Made our Elder Brother —
Will but clasp the chain of love
Closer, when we meet above.

Therefore dread I not to go
  O'er the Silent River.
Death, thy hastening oar I know;
  Bear me, thou Life-giver,
Through the waters, to the shore,
Where mine own have gone before!

MORE LIFE.

NOT weary of Thy world,
So beautiful, O Father, in Thy love,
Thy world, that, glory-lighted from above,
Lies in thy hand impearled:

Not asking rest from toil; —
Sweet toil, that draws us nearer to Thy side;
Ever to tend Thy planting satisfied,
Though in ungenial soil:

Nor to be freed from care,
That lifts us out of self's lone hollowness;
Since unto Thy dear feet we all may press,
And leave our burdens there:

But O for tireless strength!
A life untainted by the curse of sin,
That spreads no vile contagion from within; —
Found without spot, at length!

For power, and stronger will
To pour out love from the heart's inmost springs;
A constant freshness for all needy things;
In blessing, blessed still!

O to be clothed upon
With the white radiance of a heavenly form!
To feel the winged Psyche quit the worm,
Life, life eternal won!

O to be free, heart-free
From all that checks the right endeavor here!
To drop the weariness, — the pain, — the fear, —
To know death cannot be!

O but to breathe in air
Where there can be no tyrant and no slave;
Where every thought is pure, and high, and brave,
And all that is is fair!

More life! the life of heaven!
A perfect liberty to do Thy will:
Receiving all from Thee, and giving still,
Freely as Thou hast given!

More life! a prophecy
Is in that thirsty cry, if read aright.
Deep calleth unto deep: Life Infinite,
O soul, awaiteth thee!

NOTES.

NOTES.

Note 1. Page 82.

"Below, on each side of the door, are two beautiful groups. That to the right of the spectator represents Siegfried and Chriemhild. She is leaning on the shoulder of her warlike husband, with an air of the most inimitable and graceful abandonment in her whole figure: a falcon sits upon her hand, on which her eyes are turned with the most profound expression of tenderness and melancholy; she is thinking upon her dream, in which was foreshadowed the early and terrible doom of her husband." — *Mrs. Jameson.* — *Description of the new palace at Munich.*

Note 2. Page 85.

From Mrs. Jameson's "Legends of the Monastic Orders."

Note 3. Page 93.

"King Robert the Second of France was author of the touching hymn, in which all his gentle nature seems to speak: — 'Veni Sancte Spiritus.' King Robert had certainly more of the monk than the king about him. Necessity drove him to the cares and the state of royalty; but his joys were in church-music, which he composed, in devotion, and in alms-giving." — *Christian Life in Song.*

Note 4. Page 192.

Suggested by a bas-relief of the prophet Jeremiah, by Marguerite Foley, an American lady residing in Italy.

Note 5. Page 217.

"But why I went hence, and went thither, Thou knewest, O God, yet shewedst it neither to me, nor to my mother, who grievously bewailed my journey, and followed me as far as the sea. But I deceived her; and I feigned that I had a friend whom I could not leave till he had a fair wind to sail. And yet refusing to return without me, I scarcely persuaded her to stay that night in a place hard by our ship, where was an Oratory in memory of the blessed Cyprian. And what was she asking with so many tears of Thee, but that thou wouldst not suffer me to sail? But Thou, in the depth of Thy counsels, and hearing the main point of her desire, regardedst not what she then asked, that Thou mightest make me what she ever asked. The wind blew and filled our sails, and withdrew the shore from sight; and she on the morrow was there, frantic with sorrow." — *Confessions of St. Augustine.*

"For whence was that dream whereby Thou comfortedst her?— She saw herself standing on a certain wooden rule, and a shining youth coming towards her, cheerful and smiling upon her, herself grieving. But he, having inquired the cause of her grief and daily tears, told her to look and observe 'That where she was, there was I also.' And when she looked, she saw me standing by her in the same rule. When I would fain bend the vision to mean, that she rather should not despair of being one day what I was; she replied "No; for it was not told me, 'Where he, there thou also'; but, 'Where thou, there he also.'" — *Ibid.*

"She and I stood alone, leaning in a certain window which looked into the garden of the house where we now lay, at Ostia. We were discoursing then together, alone, very sweetly. . . . Such things was

I speaking, when my mother said; 'Son, for mine own part I have no further any delight in this life. What I do here any longer, and why I am here, I know not, now that my hopes in this world are accomplished. One thing there was for which I desired to linger a little while in this life, that I might see thee a Catholic Christian before I died. My God hath done this for me more abundantly: what do I here?' Scarce five days after she fell sick of a fever. On the ninth day of her sickness was that religious and holy soul freed from the body."—*Ibid.*

Note 6. Page 250.

"The Pilgrim they laid in a large upper chamber, whose window opened towards the sun-rising: the name of the chamber was Peace." —*Bunyan's Pilgrim's Progress.*

THE END.

Cambridge: Stereotyped and Printed by Welch, Bigelow, & Co.

www.ingramcontent.com/pod-product-compliance
Lightning Source LLC
LaVergne TN
LVHW010220110826
845151LV00004B/1149

9781425526634